"Rarely does one find such a rich combinat
sionate exegetical argument. This is a war
of the central claims of the Reformation. .
common heritage from the perspective of Anabaptist/Baptist distinctives that
recognizes important differences with the magisterial Reformers. For both reasons, *Why the Reformation Still Matters* represents an important contribution
to ongoing conversations in the global church."

> **Michael Horton,** J. Gresham Machen Professor of Systematic Theology
> and Apologetics, Westminster Seminary California; author, *Calvin on
> the Christian Life*

"Authors Michael Reeves and Tim Chester have made a solid contribution
to the commemoration of the Reformation in their clear account of what the
major Reformers, especially Martin Luther and John Calvin, taught about
Jesus, God's grace, Scripture, the sacraments, and other important subjects.
With the five-hundredth anniversary of Martin Luther's posting of the Ninety-
Five Theses quickly approaching, this timely book underscores the vital importance of what he and other early Protestants devoted their lives to teaching."

> **Mark Noll,** Francis A. McAnaney Professor Emeritus of History,
> University of Notre Dame; Editor, *Protestantism after 500 Years*

"Reeves and Chester clearly and straightforwardly explain the vital importance of the Reformation, summarize its message, and show its ongoing relevance. *Why the Reformation Still Matters* may be only two hundred pages
long, but it vibrates with life. A brilliant achievement by two modern-day
doctors of the church, and a great little book."

> **Sinclair B. Ferguson,** Professor of Systematic Theology, Redeemer
> Seminary, Dallas; author, *The Whole Christ*

"If there are any doubts over whether the Reformation still matters or whether
the church needs to be always reforming, Reeves and Chester dispel them.
Winsome and wise, this book provides solid reasons to be Protestant and offers
biblically and historically accurate accountings of key doctrinal formulations.
As Protestant Christians around the world celebrate the five-hundredth anniversary of the Revolution of 1517, they will find strong encouragement here.
Semper reformanda!"

> **Sean Lucas,** Professor of Church History, Reformed Theological
> Seminary, Jackson, Mississippi; Senior Minister, The First Presbyterian
> Church, Hattiesburg, Mississippi; author, *God's Grand Design:
> The Theological Vision of Jonathan Edwards*

Why the Reformation Still Matters

WHY THE *REFORMATION* STILL MATTERS

Michael Reeves and
Tim Chester

:: CROSSWAY®

WHEATON, ILLINOIS

Cover design: Matt Naylor

Cover image: Vlntn / Adobe Stock

First printing 2016

Printed in the United States of America

Scripture quotations are from the ESV® Bible (The Holy Bible, English Standard Version®), copyright © 2001 by Crossway, a publishing ministry of Good News Publishers. Used by permission. All rights reserved.

Trade paperback ISBN: 978-1-4335-4531-3
ePub ISBN: 978-1-4335-4534-4
PDF ISBN: 978-1-4335-4532-0
Mobipocket ISBN: 978-1-4335-4533-7

Library of Congress Cataloging-in-Publication Data

Names: Reeves, Michael (Michael D.), author.
Title: Why the Reformation still matters / Michael Reeves and Tim Chester.
Description: Wheaton: Crossway, 2016. | Includes bibliographical references and index.
Identifiers: LCCN 2016009209 (print) | LCCN 2016020757 (ebook) | ISBN 9781433545313 (tp) | ISBN 9781433545344 (epub) | ISBN 9781433545320 (pdf) | ISBN 9781433545337 (mobi)
Subjects: LCSH: Reformation. | Theology, doctrinal—Popular works. | Reformed Church—Doctrines.
Classification: LCC BR305.3 .R38 2016 (print) | LCC BR305.3 (ebook) | DDC 270.6—dc23
LC record available at https://lccn.loc.gov/2016009209

Crossway is a publishing ministry of Good News Publishers.

VP		26	25	24	23	22	21	20	19	18	17	16
15	14	13	12	11	10	9	8	7	6	5	4	3	2	1

In memoriam
Edward Coombs
He loved and lived for Jesus Christ.
The world was not worthy of him.

Contents

Abbreviations

Calvin, *Commentary* *Calvin's Commentaries* (New Testament).
Edited by D. W. Torrance and T. F. Torrance.
12 vols. Edinburgh: Saint Andrew Press,
1959–1972

Calvin, *Institutes* *Institutes of the Christian Religion*. Edited by
John T. McNeill. Translated by Ford Lewis
Battles. 2 vols. The Library of Christian
Classics 20–21. Philadelphia: Westminster;
London: SCM, 1961

Luther's Works *Luther's Works: American Edition*. Edited by
Jaroslav Pelikan and Helmet T. Lehmann, 55
vols. Philadelphia: Fortress; St. Louis, MO:
Concordia, 1955–1987

Introduction

Five hundred years ago a young German monk walked from his monastery, across the town of Wittenberg, to the Castle Church. The door of the church acted as a kind of public bulletin board. There the monk nailed a poster with ninety-five statements or theses. His name was Martin Luther (1483–1546). The ninety-five theses were an invitation to a public debate. It was the sixteenth-century version of a provocative blog post inviting online discussion. The prompt was the practice of the Dominican friar Johann Tetzel (1465–1519). Luther's close friend and colleague Philip Melanchthon (1497–1560) described Tetzel as "a most audacious sycophant."[1] "A brazen creep," we might say today. Most people at the time believed in purgatory, a place of torment to which people went at their death so they could be purged of their sins before moving on to heaven. Tetzel was selling indulgences—promises from the pope that gave people time off purgatory. "As soon as the coin in the coffer rings, the soul from purgatory springs" went the advertising jingle. Luther's ninety-five theses were a protest against these indulgences and the church's preoccupation with wealth. They were not a particularly radical series of statements, cer-

---

1. Philip Melanchthon, *The Life and Acts of Martin Luther* (1549), accessed February 24, 2016, http://www.iclnet.org/pub/resources/text/wittenberg/melan/lifea-01.txt.

tainly not by the standards of Luther's later thought. They did not question the existence of purgatory or even the limited value of indulgences. But they hit the church where it was most vulnerable—in the pocket.

The local archbishop complained to the pope. But the opposition made Luther more resolute. He began to attack the infallibility of the pope. He burned the papal bull that threatened his excommunication. Emperor Charles V called a conference in the city of Worms. Luther's friends ably defended him, but the emperor eventually called Luther himself to attend, with the promise of protection. Here stood Luther with the whole church system ranged against him. Luther said:

> Through the mercy of God, I ask your Imperial Majesty and your Illustrious Lordships, or anyone of any standing, to testify and refute my errors, to contradict them with the Old and New Testaments. I am ready, if better instructed, to recant any error and I shall be the first to throw my writings into the fire.

The imperial advocate responded in a chiding tone:

> Your answer is not to the point. There should be no questioning of things which the Church Councils have already condemned and on which decisions have already been passed. . . . Give us a plain reply to this question: Are you prepared to recant or not?

Luther replied:

> Your Imperial Majesty and your Lordships demand a simple answer. Here it is, plain and straight. Unless I am convicted of error by the Scriptures . . . and my conscience is taken captive by God's word, I cannot and will not recant anything, for to act against our conscience is neither safe

for us or open to us. On this I take my stand. I can do no other. God help me. Amen.[2]

Luther's ideas spread across Europe, speeded by the recently invented printing press. In many places they found a ready audience. The evident corruption of the Catholic Church had given many people a longing for change, and renewed interest in ancient learning associated with the Renaissance had led to a rediscovery of the Scriptures.

Already in the Swiss city of Zurich, Huldrych Zwingli (1484–1531) was introducing reform on the basis of his reading of the Bible, which he had come to regard as the supreme authority in all matters. At first his reforms were welcomed by the Catholic authorities, but in 1523, after two public disputations, the city backed Zwingli and broke from Rome.

In England William Tyndale (1494–1536) was influenced by Luther's ideas. Serving as a chaplain at Little Sodbury Manor, near Bath, he was shocked by the ignorance of the local clergy. To one he famously said, "If God spare my life, ere many years pass, I will cause a boy that driveth the plough shall know more of the Scriptures than thou dost."[3] Tyndale set off to London, expecting to receive church support for his plan to translate the Bible into English. But the bishop of London was not interested, because he did not want Lutheran ideas spreading in England. Opposition to Tyndale grew, and eventually he left England for life on the run in Germany and modern-day Belgium. Tyndale was eventually betrayed and martyred in 1536, but not before he had translated the New Testament and much of the Old.

---

2. Martin Luther, "The Diet of Worms: Luther's Final Answer," cited in Henry Bettenson and Chris Maunder, *Documents of the Christian Church*, 4th ed. (Oxford: Oxford University Press, 2011), 214.

3. William Tyndale, *The Works of William Tyndale*, 2 vols. (Cambridge: Parker Society, 1848; repr., Edinburgh: Banner of Truth, 2010), 1:xix.

In 1536 John Calvin (1509–1564) was passing through Geneva on his way to Strasbourg. But the leader of the church in Geneva, William Farel (1489–1565), persuaded him to stay, and the city gave him the job of teacher of Scripture. Farel was a Reformer but lacked a talent for organization. So Calvin took the lead. Initially the citizens of Geneva were not sure they liked Calvin's comprehensive vision of a Christian city, and in 1538 he was sacked. But three years later Calvin was reappointed and spent the rest of his life making Geneva a powerhouse for Reformation ideas, sending pastors across Europe to plant Reformation churches.

In England the origins of the Reformation were as much political as religious. Henry VIII (1491–1547) wanted to divorce his first wife, Catherine of Aragon (1485–1536), because she had failed to give him the son and successor he craved. But, after much prevarication, the pope refused to sanction the divorce. It did not help that the pope was beholden to Emperor Charles V, who also happened to be Catherine's nephew. So in 1534 Henry broke from Rome, making himself the head of the Church of England. Henry wanted to retain Catholic theology without Roman authority.

But, while the origins of the Reformation in England might have been political, plenty of people were sympathetic toward Luther's ideas. Henry's archbishop, Thomas Cranmer (1489–1556), was intent on Protestant reform. His prayer book, the Book of Common Prayer, wrote Reformation theology into the weekly liturgy of parish churches across England. In subsequent years England seesawed between Protestantism and Catholicism until Elizabeth I (1533–1603) settled the country on her own peculiarly English version of Protestantism (a version that rather disappointed the Puritans).

Luther posted his ninety-five theses on October 31, 1517.

The Reformation was a complex movement with many tributaries. It was not the work of one man or one movement. Nevertheless, October 31, 1517, has taken on symbolic significance. More than any other event, this has the best claim to be the starting gun that set everything else in motion. But five hundred years on, does the Reformation still matter? It matters because this is our story. If you are Anglican, Baptist, Brethren, Congregational, Independent, Lutheran, Mennonite, Methodist, Pentecostal, Presbyterian, or Reformed, then these are your roots. Your history can be traced back to these events five hundred years ago.

But are the Reformers like embarrassing grandparents? Are they a part of our story we would rather leave behind or can safely ignore? Or are they perhaps heroes we are content to lionize at a safe distance?

The sensibilities of the Reformation can certainly seem strange to modern people. Was Europe really thrown into turmoil by debates over whether righteousness was "imputed" or "imparted," the one a declaration that we are right with God and the other simply a new power to win God's approval? Did people really fight over whether we are saved by faith alone or by faith and works combined? Was there really a time when theology mattered this much to people?

Is the Reformation Bad News?

I (Tim) was watching a television documentary recently when the presenter said, "In many ways the Reformation and the bitterness and division it represents reminds us of the worst aspects of our religious instincts."[4] I can rewind my television, so I was able to check that I had heard him right. These words typify

---

4. Ifor ap Glyn, "Pagans and Pilgrims: Britain's Holiest Places," episode 1, BBC4, first broadcast March 7, 2013.

the attitude of many. Religion is a thing of mystery, people suppose. And with this supposition goes another: that to claim to know the truth and challenge other people's perception of the truth is a ridiculous act of arrogance. To quarrel about religion is uncharitable, a denial of the very thing you claim to follow.

It is certainly true that we can act toward people with whom we disagree in ways that deny the gospel we profess, and the leaders of the Reformation were sometimes guilty of this. But the assumption behind such attitudes is that the divisions of the Reformation were not worth making—truth does not really matter.

But consider what was at stake. At its heart the Reformation was a dispute about how we know God and how we can be right with him. At stake was our eternal future, a choice between heaven and hell.

And it still is. That our modern world finds the Reformation alien says as much about us as it does about the Reformers. It exposes our preoccupation with this material world and this momentary life. If there is a world beyond this world and a life beyond this life, then it does not seem to matter very much to us—out of sight, out of mind. It is a bizarre position to take when so much is at stake. For the Reformers there was no need more pressing than assurance in the face of divine judgment, and there was no act more loving than to proclaim a message of grace that granted eternal life to those who responded with faith.

The Reformation still matters because eternal life still matters.

Is the Reformation Yesterday's News?

The Reformation still matters because the debates between Catholics and Protestants have not gone away. Today there are voices claiming that the Reformation is over. Any substantial differences between Catholics and Protestants, it is claimed, have faded away or been overtaken by more pressing concerns. It makes no sense, according to this line of thinking, to live our lives as if we are still embroiled in the sixteenth century.

In 1994 a number of leading evangelicals and Roman Catholics signed a document entitled *Evangelicals and Catholics Together*. While noting ongoing differences, this controversial document called for mutual acceptance and common witness. Among the signatories was the evangelical historian Mark Noll. In 2005 he published a book (with Carolyn Nystrom) entitled *Is the Reformation Over?* The answer, he acknowledges, is complex. But Noll claims that on justification "many Catholics and evangelicals now believe approximately the same thing."[5] Although he identifies the nature of the church as an ongoing difference, Noll says:

> If it is true, as once was repeated frequently by Protestants conscious of their anchorage in Martin Luther or John Calvin that *iustificatio articulus stantis vel cadentis ecclesiae* (justification is the article on which the church stands or falls), then the Reformation is over.[6]

Highlighting numerous examples of cooperation, Noll says that differences between Catholics and evangelicals are "infinitesimal" compared with their shared differences with liberal Christianity and secular culture.[7]

Of course much has changed over the past five hundred years. On many moral issues like abortion Catholics and Prot-

---

5. Mark A. Noll and Carolyn Nystrom, *Is the Reformation Over? An Evangelical Assessment of Contemporary Roman Catholicism* (Grand Rapids, MI: Baker, 2005), 231.
6. Ibid., 232.
7. Ibid., 230.

estants find themselves making common cause. And much has changed within both Catholicism and Protestantism. Both have been impacted by modernism and postmodernism. If the differences are narrowing, it is often because many Catholics no longer follow official papal teaching, and many Protestants are losing the biblical insights gained at the Reformation. We need a stronger, not a weaker, focus on Reformation theology.

Sixteenth-century Catholics and Protestants both acknowledged they had much in common. That is not news. But they also knew the differences between them were fundamental. They could not be ignored then, and they cannot be ignored now. The fault lines of the Reformation have not gone away. Our contention is that on key issues like justification and Scripture the issues remain and are not negligible.

But it is not just in discussion with Catholicism that the Reformation continues to matter. The Reformation was always intended to be an ongoing project. One of its slogans was *semper reformanda*, usually translated as "always reforming"; but a better translation may be "always being reformed" (by God's Word). It describes not a movement forward to some uncharted horizon but a continual movement back to God's Word.

In this book we outline some key emphases of the Reformation and explore their contemporary relevance. We look at questions like How can we get God's approval? How can we overcome sin in our lives? How does God speak to us? How can we know what is true? Why do we take bread and wine? Which church should we join? What difference does God make on Monday mornings? What hope can we have in the face of death?

It is our contention that five hundred years on, evangelical churches would be well served by a rediscovery of Reformation theology. The thought of the Reformers not only challenges Catholic practice; it also challenges many aspects of evangelical practice. The Reformers are not embarrassing grandparents—they are vital conversation partners with the potential to renew and reinvigorate our churches.

1

Justification

How Can We Be Saved?

Luther's Story and Justification

The first biography of Luther was written by his friend Philip Melanchthon in 1549. Melanchthon tells us that after Luther graduated, he started to study law. His family and friends confidently expected that the bright young Luther would make a major contribution to the state, but instead he joined the Augustinian monks.

> On his entrance there, he not only applied with the closest diligence to ecclesiastical studies; but also, with the greatest severity of discipline, he exercised the government of himself, and far surpassed all others in the comprehensive range of reading and disputation with a zealous observance of fasting and prayer.[1]

---

1. Philip Melanchthon, *The Life and Acts of Martin Luther* (1549), accessed October 15, 2015, http://www.iclnet.org/pub/resources/text/wittenberg/melan/lifea-01.txt.

But all his religious endeavors could not give Luther any assurance. When a close friend died, Luther became terrified by the thought of the judgment of God. And it was all made worse by the theology of the day. Medieval theology saw sin as a problem of *being* that needed *healing*. This took place through sacraments. In this life the Christian is suspended between the grace of God (mediated through the sacraments) and the judgment of God. Medieval theology, then, added a distinction between *actual* grace and *habitual* grace. Actual grace gave forgiveness of sins, provided they were confessed. Habitual grace changed people deeper down, in their very being—overcoming the problem of original sin.

Luther's problem was that since only actual sins confessed were forgiven, he was obsessed with not overlooking sin. He would spend hours in confessing to his superior in the Augustinian order, and then come rushing back with some new misdemeanor he had remembered. At one point his superior said: "Look here, Brother Martin. If you're going to confess so much, why don't you go do something worth confessing? Kill your mother or father! Commit adultery! Stop coming in here with such flummery and fake sins!"[2]

In 1512 Luther, aged twenty-six, was sent by his order as a lecturer of biblical studies to the new university at Wittenberg. It was here, studying Augustine and lecturing on the Psalms, Romans, and Galatians, that Luther came to a radically fresh understanding of the gospel.

Sorting out the development of Luther's thought is notoriously difficult. Luther's new convictions took time to form. There is a lot of debate among scholars about what he believed and when he believed it. So we shall present it in a simplified

---

2. *Luther's Works*, 33:191, cited in Timothy George, *Theology of the Reformers* (Nashville: Broadman; Leicester: Apollos, 1988), 65.

form as a double movement. It is more complex than this, with significant overlaps, but this form will help us understand what was going on in theological terms.

Luther's First Step: Righteousness as a Gift

One key moment is what is known as Luther's "tower experience." Its date is contested, and it may have a longer process than one "eureka" moment. Luther described his experience like this:

> Meanwhile in that same year, 1519, I had begun interpreting the Psalms once again. I felt confident that I was now more experienced, since I had dealt in university courses with St. Paul's Letters to the Romans, to the Galatians, and the Letter to the Hebrews. I had conceived a burning desire to understand what Paul meant in his Letter to the Romans, but thus far there had stood in my way, not the cold blood around my heart, but that one word which is in chapter one: "The justice of God is revealed in it." I hated that word, "justice of God" (*iustitia Dei*), which, by the use and custom of all my teachers, I had been taught to understand philosophically as referring to formal or active justice, as they call it, i.e., that justice by which God is just and by which he punishes sinners and the unjust.
>
> But I, blameless monk that I was, felt that before God I was a sinner with an extremely troubled conscience. I couldn't be sure that God was appeased by my satisfaction. I did not love, no, rather I hated the just God who punishes sinners. In silence, if I did not blaspheme, then certainly I grumbled vehemently and got angry at God. I said, "Isn't it enough that we miserable sinners, lost for all eternity because of original sin, are oppressed by every kind of calamity through the Ten Commandments? Why does God heap sorrow upon sorrow through the Gospel and through the Gospel threaten us with his justice and his wrath?" This

was how I was raging with wild and disturbed conscience. I constantly badgered St. Paul about that spot in Romans 1 and anxiously wanted to know what he meant.

I meditated night and day on those words until at last, by the mercy of God, I paid attention to their context: "The justice of God is revealed in it, as it is written: 'The just person lives by faith.'" I began to understand that in this verse the justice of God is that by which the just person lives by a gift of God, that is by faith. I began to understand that this verse means that the justice of God is revealed through the Gospel, but it is a passive justice, i.e. that by which the merciful God justifies us by faith, as it is written: "The just person lives by faith." All at once I felt that I had been born again and entered into paradise itself through open gates. Immediately I saw the whole of Scripture in a different light. I ran through the Scriptures from memory and found that other terms had analogous meanings, e.g., the work of God, that is, what God works in us; the power of God, by which he makes us powerful; the wisdom of God, by which he makes us wise; the strength of God, the salvation of God, the glory of God.

I exalted this sweetest word of mine, "the justice of God," with as much love as before I had hated it with hate. This phrase of Paul was for me the very gate of paradise. Afterward I read Augustine's "On the Spirit and the Letter," in which I found what I had not dared hope for. I discovered that he too interpreted "the justice of God" in a similar way, namely, as that with which God clothes us when he justifies us. Although Augustine had said it imperfectly and did not explain in detail how God imputes justice to us, still it pleased me that he taught the justice of God by which we are justified.[3]

---

3. "Martin Luther Discovers the True Meaning of Righteousness," an excerpt from "Preface to the Complete Edition of Luther's Latin Works" (1545), trans. Andrew Thornton from "Vorrede zu Band I der Opera Latina der Wittenberger Ausgabe, 1545," in vol. 4 of *Luthers Werke in Auswahl*, ed. Otto Clemen, 6th ed. (Berlin: de Gruyter, 1967), 421–28.

In Romans 1:17 Paul writes, "For in it [the gospel] the righteousness of God is revealed from faith for faith, as it is written, 'The righteous shall live by faith.'" Luther could not understand how the righteousness or justice of God could be *gospel*—good news. It seemed to offer only the threat of judgment. Not only does the law condemn us, but so does the gospel! "For *in the gospel* a righteousness of God is revealed." But Luther began to see the righteousness of God revealed in the gospel not simply as a *quality of* God—his impartial justice by which he judges sinners. Instead he saw it as a *gift from* God. The righteousness of God is the righteousness he gives to us so that we may be righteousness before him. The righteousness of God is not an attribute of God that stands over and against humankind, judging us on the basis of merit. It is the gift of God by which God declares us righteous even though we are not in ourselves righteous. Luther says:

> [Paul] says that they are all sinners, unable to glory in God. They must, however, be justified through faith in Christ, who has merited this for us by his blood and has become for us a mercy seat [compare Ex. 25:17; Lev. 16:14–15; 1 John 2:2] in the presence of God, who forgives us all our previous sins. In so doing, God proves that it is his justice alone, *which he gives through faith*, that helps us, the justice which was at the appointed time revealed through the Gospel and, previous to that, was witnessed to by the Law and the Prophets.[4]

This first step in Luther's thought was from a troubled conscience, created by medieval theology, to a rediscovery of the view of Augustine—and Augustine's view of sin. Luther came

---

4. Martin Luther, "Preface to the Letter of St. Paul to the Romans," trans. Brother Andrew Thornton OSB, accessed October 9, 2015, www.ccel.org/ccel/luther/prefacetoromans (emphasis added); also available at www.yale.edu/adhoc/etexts/luther_preface.html.

to see sin not simply as a weakness of being or lack of good, but as rebellion against God. It was a *relational* problem. Moreover, man *coram Deo* (before God) had *no* resources. Luther said, "If anyone would feel the greatness of sin he would not be able to go on living another moment; so great is the power of sin."[5]

But Luther would go beyond Augustine. Augustine had said that when a sinner recognizes his need of salvation, he turns in faith to God. God gives him the Holy Spirit, who begins to change him. In this view of Augustine's, the righteousness of God is *the gift of transforming grace within us.* And *justification is the process of healing* which the Spirit works within us. God changes us from a selfish person into a loving person so that we can obey him from the heart. Righteousness is a gift, but it still requires a process of change from us in response.

Luther's Second Step: External Righteousness

The second step in Luther's thought moved him from Augustine's view to a distinctive evangelical position. If that first step in his thought was a rediscovery of Augustine, the second movement can be seen as a rediscovery of Paul. Luther now sees that "justify" does not mean to *make* righteous or to change a person, but to *reckon* righteous, to declare righteous, to acquit. Justification is about my *status* before God, not what God does *within* me.

Medieval theology thought of grace as a quality at work *within* us. Righteousness would be given to us so that we could become justified. We would be healed by God's grace so that we could be right before him.

---

5. D. Martin Luthers Werke: Kritische Gesamtausgabe (Weimar: Böhlau, 1833–), 39:210, cited in Paul Althaus, *The Theology of Martin Luther* (Philadelphia: Fortress, 1966), 142.

But Luther said that grace was not some "thing" at work within us, but God's unmerited favor toward us. The cause of justification is the alien righteousness of Christ. It is "alien" not because it comes from outer space(!) but because it is external to us. It is not inherent within people or in any sense said to belong to them. It is extrinsic rather than intrinsic. Luther spoke of God's accepting the righteousness of Christ as our righteousness even though it is alien to our nature. We are declared righteous not on the basis of a future gradual process of healing, but on the basis of the finished work of Christ.

Melanchthon in particular developed the idea of extrinsic righteousness into the idea of "imputation" (though Luther, too, uses the phrase in his description of his experience in the tower). Medieval theology (and the early Luther) spoke of an impartation or infusion of righteousness that effected our justification. But Melanchthon spoke of the righteousness of Christ as being "imputed" to us—it is reckoned as ours by God. Our sins are not removed but are not counted against us. Justification, then, is not about God *making* us righteous, but *declaring* us righteous. It is the language of the law court rather than the hospital. Justification is not a process of healing but a declaration that we have a right, positive standing before God.

By Faith Alone

We are declared righteous in this way by *faith alone*. Luther saw people as passive in the process of justification. We cannot initiate the process. We are powerless and enslaved. We have nothing to contribute to our salvation. And so justification is—and can only be—by faith and by faith alone. Faith, here, is *fiducia*, "personal trust or reliance." In the medieval period, faith was often seen as a virtue (in the sense of "faithfulness" or "loyalty"). For Luther faith is simply taking hold of Christ. It is receiving what Christ has done.

If anyone thinks these are subtle distinctions or that the difference with Catholicism is exaggerated, consider the statements made at the Council of Trent (1545–1563). The Council of Trent was Catholicism's response to the Reformation, a response it has never retracted. It was quite explicit in its condemnation of justification by faith alone:

> If any one says, that by faith alone the ungodly are justified in such a way as to mean that nothing else is required to co-operate in order to receive the grace of Justification and that it is not necessary for a man to be prepared and disposed by the movement of his own will; let him be anathema. (Sess. 6, Canon 9)

> If any one says that justifying faith is nothing else but confidence in the divine mercy which forgives sins for Christ's sake; or that we are justified by this confidence alone; let him be anathema. (Sess. 6, Canon 12)

The contrast to Luther is stark. Luther says, "If faith is not without all, even the smallest works, it does not justify; indeed it is not even faith."[6] Luther, as we shall see, was clear that faith goes on to produce good works in a person's life. But any hope of salvation based on good works, even in part, denies the adequacy of our only true hope, Jesus Christ.

Because in Catholicism salvation depends on faith plus works, the council denies the possibility of assurance. For the Reformers, to express assurance was to boast in Christ and his

---

6. *D. Martin Luthers Werke*, 7:231, cited in George, *Theology of the Reformers*, 71.

finished work. For Catholicism, to express assurance was a proud and presumptuous boast in your own good works.

> If any one says that a man who is born again and justified is bound by faith to believe that he is assuredly in the number of the predestinate. . . . and that he has the gift of perseverance to the end (unless he has learned this by special revelation); let him be anathema. (Sess. 6, Canons 15–16)

In recent years Catholic contributors to ecumenical discussions have made statements on justification by faith that some evangelicals have felt able to affirm. But typically these statements lack precision on the key issues of the Reformation. They fall far short of a repudiation of the anathemas against Reformation theology made at the Council of Trent.

At Once Righteous and a Sinner

At first Luther thought of Christians as partly sinful and partly righteous. The phrase in Latin is *simul iustus et peccator*, "at the same time righteous and a sinner." Luther continued to use this phrase, but understood it differently. He would add the word *semper*, "always." The Christian was *always* righteous (in status) and *always* sinful (in lifestyle). We are not in a gradual process from one thing to another. We are sinful because we continue in our old sinful habits. But we have already appeared before the judgment seat of God and have been declared righteous.

> We are in truth and totally sinners, with regard to ourselves and our first birth. Contrariwise, insofar as Christ has been given for us, we are holy and just totally. Hence from different aspects we are said to be just and sinners at one and the same time.[7]

---

7. *D. Martin Luthers Werke*, 39:523, cited in George, *Theology of the Reformers*, 71.

Summary

We may summarize Luther's theology of justification this way:

1. Justification is a forensic act by which a believer is *declared* righteous. Justification is not a process by which a person is made righteous. "Forensic" means legal—it invokes the image of a law court. It involves a change of status—not a change of nature.

2. The cause of justification is the alien righteousness of Christ. It is not inherent within a person or in any sense said to belong to us. It is "imputed" or reckoned to us. It is not "imparted" or poured into us.

3. Justification is by faith alone. We can contribute nothing. Christ has achieved everything for us already.

4. Because justification is an act of God and because it is based on the finished work of Christ, we can have assurance. Justification is future in orientation: it is acquittal on the day of judgment. But justification is the assurance in the present that the final verdict will be in our favor.

Lutheran View of Justification	Catholic View of Justification
a forensic act	a healing act
the image of a law court	the image of a hospital
alien righteousness (of Christ)	inherent righteousness (within the believer)
imputed	imparted
by faith alone	begun with faith and continued through sacraments and good works
justified now on the basis of Christ's finished work	justified now on the basis of what we shall become
an assured future	an uncertain future

Justification and Sanctification

Erasmus, the great humanist scholar, objected to all this, saying, "Lutherans seek only two things—wealth and wives . . . to them the gospel means the right to live as they please."[8] In other words, all this talk of justification by faith alone was simply an excuse to live a decadent life. However, Luther would argue strongly that, while we are not *justified* by works, works should follow faith as its fruit. Saving faith will always be active in love. And this love is not expressed in religious duties to earn merit before God, but in practical service of one's neighbor. We are freed from the burden of self-justification to serve one another in love. In the medieval system you sought justification by retreating from the world into a monastery to spend your time in confession and religious discipline. Justification by faith meant you were free to go out into the world and spend your time serving others without always looking over your shoulder to wonder what God was thinking of you.

There were some differences among the Reformers. Melanchthon and later Lutheranism made a sharp distinction between justification and sanctification (here "sanctification" is the theological term for our growth in holiness and our gradual transformation into the image of Christ). They wanted to guard against the Catholic idea that justification begins with regeneration and is completed through sanctification. Luther himself does not make quite such a sharp distinction. Martin Bucer (1491–1551), the Swiss theologian and one of the shapers of the Reformed tradition, thought of a "double justification": first, in "primary justification" we are *declared* righteous through the imputed righteousness of Christ, and, second, through

---

8. P. S. Allen and H. M. Allen, eds., *Opus Epistolarum Des. Erasmi Roterodami* (Oxford: Oxford University Press, 1928), 7:366, letter (no. 1977) of March 20, 1528, to Willibald Pirckheimer, cited in George, *Theology of the Reformers*, 72.

"secondary justification" we are *made* righteous—an activity that includes human effort.

John Calvin—the main shaper of the Reformed tradition—had a clear concept of forensic or legal justification. But he avoided the sharp distinction between justification and sanctification (or secondary justification) by placing both under the overarching and prior concept of the union of the believer with Christ through faith. So, although he calls justification the "main hinge upon which religion turns" and the "sum of all piety,"[9] Calvin deals with justification in the *Institutes* under the topic of the Holy Spirit. Justification and sanctification are both fruit that flow from our union with Christ, which we experience through the Spirit. Calvin thus recovers the relational dimension of Luther while protecting the legal nature of justification made explicit in Melanchthon.

Does Justification Still Matter?

So, does justification still matter? The answer must be a resounding *yes*. Nothing matters more than justification by Christ alone through faith alone. If justification by faith seems obvious to you, then it is because of Luther. But we must not presume on his legacy.

Many attempts have been made to move the center ground of Christianity elsewhere. But the fact remains that the biggest problem facing humanity is God's justice. God is committed to judging sin. And that means he is committed to judging *my* sin. This is our biggest problem because that means an eternity excluded from the glory of God.

This is Paul's argument in Romans 1:18–3:20. Step by step Paul establishes that all are guilty. Romans 2:5 says, "Because

---

9. Calvin, *Institutes*, 3.11.1, 3.15.7.

of your hard and impenitent heart you are storing up wrath for yourself on the day of wrath when God's righteous judgment will be revealed." He reaches his conclusion in Romans 3:20: "For by works of the law no human being will be justified in his [God's] sight, since through the law comes knowledge of sin." Christianity brings many blessings. It is right that Christians be involved in the pursuit of neighborhood renewal and social justice. But if one day God's righteous judgment will be revealed, if in the meantime we are storing up God's wrath against ourselves, if no one can be declared righteous through his or her own righteousness, then every person on earth faces a massive problem: God's judgment. And this problem dwarfs all the other problems we face. Nothing matters more than justification.

This is why Luther described justification as "the summary of Christian doctrine" and "the article by which the church stands or falls."[10]

But it is not just at a doctrinal or ecclesial level that it matters. It is a deeply personal doctrine. Every time I sin, I create a reason to doubt my acceptance by God, and I question my future with God. But day after day the doctrine of justification speaks peace to my soul.

This is especially true of imputed righteousness. If justification describes a process of change, as Catholicism teaches, albeit one initiated by grace, then every setback throws my future into doubt. But if I am made right with God through the finished work of Christ, then nothing can unfinish that reality. I can have assurance, even in the face of my sin.

---

10. Douglas J. Moo, *The Epistle to the Romans* (Grand Rapids, MI: Eerdmans, 1996), 242, says that later Lutherans coined this slogan and that Luther had said, "If that article stands, the church stands; if it falls, the church fails" (Martin Luther, exposition of Ps. 130:4).

Paul brings his argument for justification by faith in Romans 1–4 to a climax in 4:25: "[Jesus our Lord] was delivered up for our trespasses and raised for our justification." What does he say next? What is the consequence of our justification? Paul continues: "Therefore, since we have been justified by faith, we have peace with God through our Lord Jesus Christ. Through him we have also obtained access by faith into this grace in which we stand, and we rejoice in hope of the glory of God" (Rom. 5:1–2). Justification is the reminder that we have peace with God and the hope of glory. And we need that reminder not just on the day of our conversion, but day after day.

The people of this world are on a mission: a mission to prove themselves. Perhaps the biggest reason why people are too busy is that they are trying to prove themselves. Busyness has become a mark of honor in our culture. Take an expression like "I'm a very busy man." What does it mean in our culture? It does not mean "My life's out of control." It means "I'm a very important person—you should show me some respect." The result is a level of overwork that is damaging our health and our homes.

We do not need the five hundredth anniversary of the Reformation to speak to people of justification. Every day you will meet people who are trying to prove themselves. Some are trying to prove themselves to God. Many are trying to prove themselves to others to establish their own identity. All these futile attempts at self-justification are stretching people to the breaking point.

Into this frenzy Jesus says, "Come to me . . . and I will give you rest" (Matt. 11:28). We have good news for our busy culture. Proving yourself is just another term for justifying yourself. And we have good news of justification by grace.

If you are busy trying to prove yourself, then you will always be busy. You will never get the job done—because you cannot prove yourself. You will be like a dog chasing its tail. Jesus said on the cross, "It is finished" (John 19:30). The job is done. The task is complete. There is full atonement. There is nothing left for you to do.

Justification in Evangelical Hymnody

The huge importance of justification for evangelical Christians can be seen in its prominence in evangelical worship and hymnody. Again and again throughout history you see evangelicals turning the Reformation doctrine of justification by Christ through faith alone into worship. In each case, it is quite clear, justification is not simply a doctrine to demarcate the true church. Nor is it merely a doctrine to be preached to unbelievers. It is the source of comfort and hope in the midst of the struggles of life.

We are spoiled for choice here, but take, for example, "Jesus, Your Blood and Righteousness," by Nicholas Von Zinzendorf (1700–1760), translated by John Wesley (1703–1791):

Jesus, your blood and righteousness
my beauty are, my glorious dress;
mid flaming worlds, in these arrayed
with joy shall I lift up my head.

When from the dust of death I rise
to claim my home beyond the skies
then this shall be my only plea:
Jesus has lived and died for me.

Bold shall I stand in that great day
and none condemn me, try who may;
fully absolved by you I am
from sin and fear, from guilt and shame.

O let the dead now hear your voice;
let those once lost in sin rejoice!
Their beauty this, their glorious dress,
Jesus, your blood and righteousness.

John Wesley's brother Charles (1707–1788) expressed just the same delight in our justification in his famous hymn "And Can It Be":

No condemnation now I dread;
Jesus, and all in Him, is mine!
Alive in Him, my living Head,
And clothed in righteousness divine,
Bold I approach the eternal throne,
And claim the crown, through Christ my own.

Or, finally, take "My Hope Is Built on Nothing Less," by Edward Mote (1797–1874). Like the others, it beautifully captures the confidence we can have before God in Christ, as opposed to our own performance:

My hope is built on nothing less
than Jesus' blood and righteousness;
I dare not trust the sweetest frame,
but wholly lean on Jesus' name.
On Christ, the solid Rock, I stand;
all other ground is sinking sand . . .

When I shall launch in worlds unseen,
O may I then be found in him!
Dressed in his righteousness alone,
faultless to stand before the throne.
On Christ, the solid Rock, I stand;
all other ground is sinking sand.

2

Scripture

How Does God Speak to Us?

In June 1519 Martin Luther traveled to Leipzig to debate his emerging ideas with one of the leading theologians of the Catholic Church, Johann Eck. It was more of a public debate than a trial. Nevertheless, Luther was accompanied by two hundred students armed with battle-axes. What, if anything, they planned to do with their axes is unclear!

Eck accused Luther of advocating the views of John Hus. Hus had been condemned a hundred years before at the Council of Constance and burned at the stake. Luther kept protesting that he was not like Hus, and Eck kept pressing him. Then the proceedings broke for lunch.

During the lunch break Luther went to the university library to mug up on Hus. He examined the record of the council and discovered, to his surprise, that Eck was right—he was advocating the same position as Hus.

So at the beginning of the afternoon session, to everyone's astonishment, Luther declared, "Among the articles of John Hus, I find many which are plainly Christian and evangelical which the universal Church cannot condemn."[1] Duke George, who was presiding over the debate, blurted out, "The plague." Some supporters of Hus had rampaged through George's lands in retaliation for Hus's execution. George did not want a repeat of that.

It was a dramatic moment and Luther was certainly not above a bit of melodrama. But it exemplified the problem Luther was increasingly facing. Eck had been clever. He had not taken Luther on in a debate about the meaning of the New Testament. Perhaps he suspected he would lose that debate. Instead he argued that Luther was aligning himself with someone the church had condemned as a heretic. He made it an issue of church authority. This exposed Luther's dilemma. Luther had started out wanting to reform the Catholic Church. But Eck had shown that Luther was advocating a position which the church had condemned. So for Luther the authority of the church and the authority of the Scriptures were in direct confrontation. He had to choose between them. He chose Scripture.

The debate continued with Eck saying that Hus was a heretic and Luther saying that not everything which Hus held was condemned as heretical. Eventually Luther cut to the chase: "Let me talk German. I am being misunderstood by the people. I assert that a council has sometimes erred and may sometimes err. Nor has a council authority to establish new articles of faith." Eck replied, "Are you the only one that knows anything? Except for you is all the Church in error?" Luther replied:

---

1. *D. Martin Luthers Werke: Kritische Gesamtausgabe* (Weimar: Böhlau, 1833–), 2:279, cited in Roland Bainton, *Here I Stand: Martin Luther* (Oxford: Lion, 1978), 115–16.

I answer, that God once spoke through the mouth of an ass. I will tell you straight what I think. I am a Christian theologian, and I am bound, not only to assert, but to defend the truth with my blood and death. I believe freely and will be a slave to the authority of no one, whether council, university, or pope.[2]

After eighteen days the duke George brought the debate to an end. It was not making any progress, and he wanted the hall for the entertainment of a distinguished guest who would soon be arriving. The debate continued in the form of pamphlets. By February 1520 Luther had done more research on Hus. He concluded, "We are all Hussites without knowing it."[3] With this declaration the authority of church tradition was shattered. The institutional church had condemned Hus for views that Luther now saw to be taught in God's Word.

This is the meaning of *sola Scriptura*, "Scripture alone"— one of the key slogans of the Reformation. It does not mean that other things cannot inform our theology. The Reformers quoted past theologians freely as authoritative guides. They reflected on experience and used their reason. What *sola Scriptura* does mean is that when we have to choose, there is only one choice we can make: Scripture alone is our ultimate authority. And in particular it is the supreme authority, in contrast to the authority of the church and its traditions. The Catholic Church claimed the right to interpret the Scriptures. It was the Scriptures together with the interpretation of the church that carried authority.

This is still the claim of the Catholic Church. The *Catechism of the Catholic Church* is the official contemporary statement

---

2. *D. Martin Luthers Werke*, 2:404, cited in Bainton, *Here I Stand*, 116–19.
3. *D. Martin Luthers Werke*, *Briefwechsel*, 254, cited in Bainton, *Here I Stand*, 120.

of Catholic belief, published in 1992 with the approval of Pope John Paul II.[4] The *Catechism* explicitly says that divine revelation comes in "two modes of transmission": Sacred Scripture and Holy Tradition (§81).

> As a result the Church, to whom the transmission and interpretation of Revelation is entrusted, does not derive her certainty about all revealed truths from the holy Scriptures alone. Both Scripture and Tradition must be accepted and honoured with equal sentiments of devotion and reverence. (§82)

It also goes on to say, "The task of interpreting the Word of God authentically has been entrusted solely to the Magisterium of the Church, that is, to the Pope and to the bishops in communion with him" (§100).

It was to these claims that the Reformers raised the challenge of *sola Scriptura*. It is often said that justification by faith alone was the *material principle* of the Reformation. That is, faith alone was at the heart of the *content* of the Reformation. But the recovery of Scripture was its *formal principle*. In other words, Scripture alone was at the heart of its *method*. Alister McGrath says, "If the Reformers dethroned the pope, they enthroned scripture."[5]

We often go forward by going back. And this is what happened at the Reformation. The Reformers were not trying to forge something new. They were not setting out to change the world. All they wanted to do was go back to the Bible. But going back to the Bible changed the world. This is how Luther described the Reformation:

---

4. *Catechism of the Catholic Church* (London: Geoffrey Chapman, 1994), accessed October 6, 2015, http://www.vatican.va/archive/ccc/index.htm.
5. Alister McGrath, *Reformation Thought: An Introduction* (Oxford: Blackwell, 1988), 95.

I opposed indulgences and all the papists, but never with force. I simply taught, preached, and wrote God's word; otherwise I did nothing. And while I slept, or drank Wittenberg beer with Philip and Amsdorf [Luther's friends], the word so greatly weakened the papacy that no prince or emperor ever inflicted such losses upon it. I did nothing; the word did everything.[6]

Back to the Sources

At the beginning of the medieval period most theologians and church leaders saw the Bible as the only reliable source of Christian truth. Where Scripture was silent, people could attempt to work out the implications of Scripture. But these judgments were always secondary to Scripture itself. But during the fourteenth and fifteenth centuries a different understanding of tradition developed, Tradition with a capital *T*. It assumed an unwritten Tradition going back to the first apostles that supplements the Bible and provides authoritative truth on issues on which the Bible is silent. In response to the Reformation, the Roman Catholic Council of Trent declared in 1546, "All saving truths and rules of conduct . . . are contained in the written books *and in the unwritten traditions,* . . . received by the Apostles from the mouth of Christ Himself, or from the Apostles themselves."[7] It was not always clear whether this Tradition lay with the councils of the church or with the pope, though over time the pope emerged as the key arbiter of truth.

When the medieval church talked about Scripture, it meant the *textus vulgatus,* "the common text." This was the Latin translation of the Bible by Jerome in the fourth and fifth

6. *Luther's Works,* 51:76–77.
7. Sess. 4 (emphasis added), accessed February 25, 2016, http://www.american catholictruthsociety.com/docs/TRENT/trent4.htm.

centuries. Today we call it "the Vulgate," although that term was not used until the sixteenth century.

The problem was, there were many versions of the Vulgate. Until the invention of the printing press, books were copied by hand, and so discrepancies crept in. In 1226 a "Paris Version" of the Vulgate was produced. It was a commercial venture without any ecclesiastical backing. It also contained obvious mistakes. But despite this, it soon became the normative text. McGrath says, "Medieval theologians, attempting to base their theology upon scripture, were obliged to equate scripture with a rather bad commercial edition of an already faulty Latin translation of the Bible."[8] In England John Wycliffe (ca. 1330–1384) produced an English Bible so ordinary people had access to the Scriptures. But even this was a translation from the Latin Vulgate.

All of this might not have made much difference were it not for the rise of the humanist movement. Renaissance humanism was very different from modern humanism. Modern humanism is the belief that human beings can solve their own problems and develop their own ethics without outside help from the likes of God. Renaissance humanism was a recovery of Greek and Roman thought. The slogan was *ad fontes*, "back to the sources." It was driven by a passion to read accurate versions of classical texts in their original languages—including the Bible.

In 1516 Erasmus, acknowledged as the greatest humanist scholar of them all, published a Greek version of the New Testament. And this would prove to be a key development for what became the Reformation. Consider this passage: "From that time on Jesus began to preach, 'Do penance, for the kingdom of heaven is near.'" You are probably not familiar with this

---

8. McGrath, *Reformation Thought*, 98.

version of Matthew 4:17. And for good reason. It is not what Matthew wrote. But it is what the Vulgate says (albeit in Latin). Erasmus was able to show that, instead of referring to a sacrament of penance, Jesus was talking about a radical change of direction. "Do penance" should be translated "repent." Or again, the Vulgate describes Mary as "full of grace." It implies that Mary was like a reservoir of grace that devout Christians could access. As we shall see, for medieval Catholicism grace was like a can of the energy drink Red Bull, which pumps us up spiritually. Extending this analogy, Mary became a drinks dispenser. But Erasmus said that Luke 1:28 should really be translated "favored one." Mary was not a *dispenser* of grace, but a *recipient* of grace—just like us.

As humanism got to work, the holes in medieval Catholic theology were being exposed, and light was beginning to shine through. John Calvin concluded:

> Let this be a firm principle: No other word is to be held as the Word of God, and given place as such in the church, than what is contained first in the Law and the Prophets, then in the writings of the apostles: and the only authorized way of teaching in the church is by the prescription and standard of his Word.[9]

Calvin's words highlight another distinctive of the Reformation. If you compare the Vulgate or a modern Catholic Bible in English (like the Jerusalem Bible) with the New International Version or English Standard Version, you will immediately notice the Catholic version has some extra books between the Old and New Testaments. These are known as the "Apocrypha."

---

9. Calvin, *Institutes*, 4.8.8.

One Catholic practice that the Reformers could not stomach was that of praying for the dead. It ran contrary to all their teaching on the need for personal faith. The Catholics claimed scriptural support because of a reference to it in 2 Maccabees 12:40–46. If you are wondering whether Maccabees is a minor prophet that you have somehow managed to miss, then do not panic. It is in the Apocrypha.

The apocryphal books were found in Greek and Latin versions of the Old Testament but not in Hebrew versions, because they had been added later. The Reformers recognized that they had some devotional value (like any other Christian book). But they were convinced that they were not part of God's Word as God has originally given it to his people.

The Rule of Christ in His Word

The Reformers believed in the authority of the historic church. They did not want a rampant individualism in which all interpretations of Scripture are equally valid. Instead they valued the history of the interpretation of Scripture. Calvin, for example, often quotes key figures from the early church as authoritative guides who support his position. The Reformers accepted the early councils and creeds of the church.

But the authority of the church, its leaders, and its councils was derived from Scripture and was therefore subordinate to Scripture. If push ever came to shove, Scripture would win every time.

The Reformers also believed in the ongoing authority of the church. But, again, this authority was tied to God's Word. It is not the office of a pastor that gives him his authority. His authority comes from God's Word. In other words, in preaching or in pastoral work he has authority as he teaches God's Word.

This led to a redefinition of a true church, as we shall see. The Catholic Church defines the church in terms of *institutional continuity*—your bishop was appointed by a bishop who was appointed by another bishop, and so on. It was all about being able to trace a family line back to Peter in Rome. But the Reformers said that what defines a true church is *gospel continuity*. Does what it preaches align with the Bible? The marks of a true church are the Word and the sacraments. The church does not establish the authenticity of the gospel. The gospel establishes the authenticity of the church. Commenting on 1 Timothy 3:15 Calvin says:

> The difference between us and the papists is that they believe that the church cannot be the pillar of the truth unless she presides over the Word of God. We, on the other hand, assert that it is *because* she reverently subjects herself to the Word of God that the truth is preserved by her, and passed on to others by her hands.[10]

Writing to the senate and people of Prague, Luther sympathizes with their nervousness about overturning the long-standing customs of the church. But he says:

> If you are troubled and anxious as to whether or not you are truly a church of God, I would say to you, that a church is not known by customs but by the Word. In 1 Cor. 14[:24–25], Paul says that if an unbeliever comes into the church and finds those disclosing the secrets of his heart, he will fall on his face and declare that God is really present there. Of this you can be sure, that the Word of God and knowledge of Christ are richly present among you. And wherever the Word of God and knowledge of Christ are,

---

10. Cited in McGrath, *Reformation Thought*, 105.

they are not in vain, however deficient those who have the Word may be in external customs.[11]

Sausages tested the authority of Scripture in Zurich. It was Lent, 1522. Traditionally only vegetables and fish were eaten during Lent. But this year twelve friends gathered for a sausage-themed party. The city council took action as they had always done and fined the host, Froschauer, albeit a nominal amount. Seven days later Zwingli produced a pamphlet (on Froschauer's printing press) in which he argued that the Bible does not say anything about eating sausages in Lent.

Of course the issue was not really about sausages. It was about the authority of Scripture and the validity of reform. A debate known as "the First Zurich Disputation" was called the following year on a variety of reforming theses. Zwingli won the day. But in some ways the debate was won before it even started because the issue at stake was whether Zwingli's ideas were in accordance with Scripture. Whatever else might be decided, it was already clear that Scripture was the authority that would determine what was right. Christ rules through his Word.

In the summer of 1522 Zwingli gained access to the Oeten-bach convent, a source of considerable influence on the religious life of Zurich. It seems some of the nuns were persuaded, and the convent was dissolved by the city council two years later. One of the sermons Zwingli preached to the nuns was published as "Of the Clarity and Certainty of the Word of God."[12]

Zwingli starts this work with the fact that human beings are made in the image of God. Because we are created for fellow-

---

11. Luther, *Concerning the Ministry* (1523), in *Luther's Works*, 40:41.
12. Huldrych Zwingli, "Of the Clarity and Certainty of the Word of God," in *Zwingli and Bullinger*, ed. G. W. Bromiley, Library of Christian Classics 24 (Louisville: Westminster John Knox, 1953), 49–95. Specific page citations will be made parenthetically in the text.

ship with God "there is nothing which can give greater joy or
assurance or comfort to the soul than the Word of its creator
and maker" (68). This is why the clarity and infallibility of the
Word are such important topics.

Zwingli first asserts the certainty or power of God's Word:

> The Word of God is so sure and strong that, if God wills, all
> things are done the moment that he speaks his Word. For it
> is so living and powerful that . . . things both rational and
> irrational are fashioned and despatched and constrained in
> conformity with its purpose. (68)

The proof of this is found in the opening verses of the Bible,
where God creates all things out of nothing through his word.
Zwingli goes on to list a few other examples of God's powerful word just from the opening chapters of Genesis. We find
the same pattern in the New Testament. Speaking of the virgin
birth, Zwingli says, "The whole course of nature must be al-
tered rather than that the Word of God should not remain and
be fulfilled" (70). He then gives example after example of the
power of the words of Jesus and the apostles "to show that the
Word of God is so alive and strong and powerful that all things
have necessarily to obey it" (71).

> The whole teaching of the Gospel is a sure demonstration
> that what God has promised will certainly be performed.
> For the Gospel is now an accomplished fact: the One who
> was promised to the patriarchs, and to the whole race, has
> now been given to us, and in him we have the assurance of
> all our hope. (72)

The point is that the word we read or hear is the same word we
see working with such power in the stories of the Bible and in
its central story, the gospel.

But Zwingli's main concern is the clarity of God's Word. That is because he is refuting the claim of the Catholic Church that the Bible needs to be interpreted by the church. There may be times when the Bible is hard to understand, but it is not written in some kind of spiritual code. Nor do we need special insiders, like priests, to interpret it for us.

Zwingli jumps straight in by refuting the objection that, if God wanted to be clear, he would not have taught in parables and riddles. Zwingli has in mind passages like Isaiah 6:9–10 and Matthew 13:10–16, which speak of Jesus's using parables so that "seeing they do not see, and hearing they do not hear" (13:13). Zwingli replies that proverbs and parables are not attempts to hide the truth. Rather God is teaching us in "a gentle and attractive way." They provoke us to search out their meaning so that "we value it more highly than if it had been presented to us plainly." "The truth which is discovered is received the more firmly and valued the more highly, and the divine lesson is busy and active all the longer in the understanding, and its roots sink deeper into the heart" (73). So God uses parables and proverbs to enlighten those "having a mind to learn from the Word of God." They mask the truth only from the person "who comes to the Scriptures with his own opinion and interpretation and wrests the Scriptures into conformity with it" (74).

Zwingli invites us to think of a good wine. To a healthy person it tastes great and warms the heart. But someone with a fever will find it distasteful and wonder how the healthy person can bear to drink it. This is not the fault of the wine, but of the sickness. In the same way, the proclamation of God's Word is always good. If people cannot bear or understand it, then the fault lies in the sickness of their souls.

Zwingli's key concern is to celebrate the clarity of the Word.

"When the Word of God shines on the human understanding, it enlightens it in such a way that it understands and confesses the Word and knows the certainty of it" (75). He cites Psalm 119:130:

> The unfolding of your words gives light;
>   it imparts understanding to the simple.

This reference to "the simple" is important for Zwingli. He is keen to refute any suggestion that we should submit to councils of bishops. God reveals himself not to those who are hungry for power or prestige but to his humble children. Is it arrogant to claim that we can interpret the Bible? Not at all, says Zwingli, for we are not relying on ourselves to gain understanding, but humbly submitting to God's Word.

Zwingli follows this up with examples from the Bible "to show conclusively that God's Word can be understood by a man without any human direction" because of "the light and Spirit of God, illuminating and inspiring the words" (78). In other words, people do not need human interpreters to understand God's Word. Indeed Zwingli's first example, Noah, obeyed God's Word *despite* human interpreters who claimed he was deluded. Zwingli then cites passages that speak of God's teaching people directly, without the need of human mediation (John 6:45; 1 Cor. 2:12–13; Heb. 8:10; 10:16; 1 John 2:27).

But how can we know our understanding is from God unless it is confirmed by the church? Zwingli replies:

> You believe that men can give you certainty, which is no certainty, and you do not believe that God can give it you. Do you not know that the mind and understanding of every man must be brought into captivity to the obedience and service of God, and not of men? (83)

In other words, we must obey God rather than people. "It is not for us to sit in judgment on Scripture and divine truth, but to let God do his work in and through it, for it is something which we can learn only of God" (92).

Another problem with saying we need the guidance of the church is that the church does not speak with one voice.

> The seeking soul cries out: Alas! whom shall I follow? They all argue so persuasively that I am at a loss what to do. And finally it can only run to God and earnestly pray to him, saying . . . "Oh God, they all disagree amongst themselves; but you are the only, unconcealed good; show me the way of salvation." And the Gospel gives us a sure message, or answer, or assurance. Christ stands before you with open arms, inviting you and saying (Matt. 11[:28]): "Come unto me, all ye that labour and are heavy laden, and I will give you rest." O glad news, which brings with it its own light, so that we know and believe that it is true. (84)

But what about when Christians disagree? Surely then someone must decide between competing interpretations? Zwingli's main complaint is that, again, this tries "to subject the doctrine of God to the judgment of men." But he also argues that, when it comes to the central message of the gospel, God's Word is clear. God's "words have always a true and natural sense; may God grant it, no matter how we may wrest them this way or that" (86). The problems arise because "rascals . . . pick out verses from it without regard to their context, and wrest them according to [their] own desire" (87)

> Alas! here we come upon the canker at the heart of all human systems. And it is this: we want to find support in Scripture for our own view, and so we take that view to Scripture, and if we find a text which, however artifi-

cially, we can relate to it, we do so, and in that way we wrest Scripture in order to make it say what we want it to say. (88)

Zwingli says that taking verses out of context "is like breaking off a flower from its roots and trying to plant it in a garden." It does not work. Instead, "you must plant it with the roots and the soil in which it is embedded" (87). In other words, disagreements can be resolved by going back to the Bible and reading the natural sense of the text in its context.

But is it not better to depend on lots of interpreters rather than just one? Zwingli would no doubt accept the wisdom of this as a practice. He is not against consulting commentaries. But he refuses to make it a rule. He argues:

> If that is the case, then Christ himself was in error, which God forbid, for most of the priests of the time held quite a different view and he had to stand alone. And the apostles were also mistaken, for they were opposed by whole nations and cities. . . . Truth is not necessarily with the majority. (87)

Zwingli does not despise the role of preachers and teachers. Indeed he says, "If he teaches you in accordance with the Word of God, it is not he that teaches you, but God who teaches him." But he also warns, "If he teaches you in accordance with his own thought and mind his teaching is false" (90).

What if I do not find myself enlightened when I read the Bible? First, Zwingli calls us to humble ourselves lest we be among those who, "though hearing, they do not hear." Then he invites us to pray for the enlightenment of God's Spirit as we read God's Word. How, then, should we approach the Scriptures?

Before I say anything or listen to the teaching of man, I will first consult the mind of the Spirit of God: "I will hear what God the Lord will speak." [Ps. 85:8] Then you should reverently ask God for his grace, that he may give you his mind and Spirit, so that you will not lay hold of your own opinion but of his. And have a firm trust that he will teach you a right understanding, for all wisdom is of God the Lord. And then go to the written word of the Gospel. (88–89)

Zwingli's conclusion is this:

The Word of God is certain and can never fail. It is clear, and will never leave us in darkness. It teaches its own truth. It arises and irradiates the soul of man with full salvation and grace. It gives the soul sure comfort in God. It humbles it, so that it loses and indeed condemns itself and lays hold of God. (93)

The Presence of Christ in His Word

What is God's Word? There is more than one answer. The first answer is that Jesus is the Word of God (capital W if you like). Second, the Bible is the word of God. The Bible is the word of God for three reasons. First, the Bible is *from God the Father*. It is a revelation of God the Father. Second, the Bible is *about God the Son*. It is the record of the Word of God in the person of Jesus, promised in the Old Testament and attested in the New Testament. Third, the Bible is *by God the Spirit*. It is the *Spirit-inspired* record of the Word of God in the person of Jesus. The Spirit ensures that it is an accurate and reliable account of the word of God. So it is from God, about God, and by God.

For the Reformers the Bible and Christ went together. We are saved by Christ alone. But we encounter Christ in the Bible. Indeed the two are linked. Christ is the incarnate Word and the

Bible is the written word. The Bible is the word of God because through the Spirit it testifies to the incarnate Word. So Christ is central to the Bible. And Christ is central to the interpretation of the Bible. All true interpretations of the Bible lead us to Jesus. But the theologians of the Reformation went further. The Second Helvetic Confession, chapter 1, has a subheading, "The Preaching of the Word of God Is the Word of God." The confession was written by Heinrich Bullinger for the Swiss Reformed Church and has become one of the key statements of faith among Reformed churches. Here is what it says under this heading:

> Wherefore when this Word of God is now preached in the church by preachers lawfully called, we believe that *the very Word of God is proclaimed, and received by the faithful*; and that neither any other Word of God is to be invented nor is to be expected from heaven: and that now the Word itself which is preached is to be regarded, not the minister that preaches; for even if he be evil and a sinner, nevertheless the Word of God remains still true and good. (emphasis added)

The idea that preaching is God's word was based on the Reformers' understanding of mission. They saw mission as an integral part of God's plan of salvation. Luther says: "Even if Christ were given for us and crucified a thousand times, it would all be vain if the Word of God were absent and were not distributed and given to me with the bidding, This is for you, take what is yours."[13] Salvation is achieved through the cross and resurrection. But it is *distributed* through the Word and by the Spirit. Without this distribution no one would be saved. Calvin, too, says that God "ordained his word as the instru-

---

13. Luther, "Against the Heavenly Prophets in the Manner of Images and Sacraments" (1525), in *Luther's Works*, 40:213.

ment by which Jesus Christ, with all his graces, is dispensed to us."[14] As such, preaching is a redemptive act.

Calvin says that God could "thunder from the sky." But if he did "we would be totally lost." Indeed there was a time when God thundered from heaven. At Sinai the Israelites heard his voice. And what happened? They trembled with fear and begged Moses to speak on God's behalf (Exodus 19–20). So Calvin speaks of God's "overflowing paternal goodness" in choosing "to teach us intimately by those who are like us."[15]

The Voice of Christ

This means that when the Word of God is preached, we hear God's voice. Luther says:

> Would to God that we would gradually train our hearts to believe that the preacher's words are God's Word. . . . It is not an angel or a hundred thousand angels but the Divine Majesty Himself that is preaching there. To be sure, I do not hear this with my ears or see it with my eyes; all I hear is the voice of the preacher . . . and I behold only a man before me. But I view the picture correctly if I add that the voice and words of [the] pastor are not his own words and doctrine but those of our Lord and God. It is not a prince, a king, or an archangel whom I hear; it is He who declares that He is able to dispense the water of eternal life.[16]

Calvin says, "Christ acts by [ministers] in such a manner that he wishes their *mouth* to be reckoned as his *mouth*, and their *lips* as his *lips*; that is, when they speak from his mouth,

---

14. John Calvin, "Short Treatise on the Supper of Our Lord," in *Selected Works of John Calvin: Tracts and Letters*, ed. and trans. Henry Beveridge, vol. 2 (Edinburgh: Calvin Translation Society, 1849; repr., Grand Rapids, MI: Baker, 1983), 166.

15. *John Calvin's Sermons on 2 Samuel: Chapters 1–13*, trans. Douglas Kelly (Edinburgh: Banner of Truth, 1992), 302.

16. Luther, "Sermons on the Gospel of St. John," in *Luther's Works*, 22:526–27.

and faithfully declare his word."[17] He then cites Luke 10:16: "The one who hears you hears me, and the one who rejects you rejects me, and the one who rejects me rejects him who sent me." When Jesus describes himself as the Good Shepherd, he says, "The sheep follow him, for they know his voice" (John 10:4). Calvin comments, "Although He is here speaking of ministers, He wants not so much them, as God speaking through them, to be heard."[18]

The Presence of Christ

The Reformers went further still. Imagine a small girl waking up in the middle of the night. She cries out for her father. It is dark. She is confused. She is frightened. And then she hears the voice of her father: "It's all right, Sweetheart. Everything's OK. You go back to sleep." The voice of her father is a reassurance of his presence.

In the same way, the Reformers said that the voice of God in the Word of God is a sign of his presence. We not only hear God's voice in his Word; we experience his presence. Consider these quotes from Calvin (emphases added):

> If our Lord is so good to us as to have his doctrine still preached to us, we have by that *a sure and infallible sign that he is near at hand to us*, that he seeks our salvation, that he calls us to himself *as though he spoke with open mouth, and that we see him personally before us*. . . . [Jesus Christ] *holds out his arms to receive us*, as often as the gospel is preached to us. . . . Let us assure ourselves that *God offers himself to us in the person of his only Son*, when he sends us pastors and teachers.[19]

---

17. Calvin, *Commentary*, on Isa. 11:4.
18. Calvin, *Commentary*, on John 10:4.
19. John Calvin, sermon on Eph. 4:11–12, in *Sermons on the Epistle to the Ephesians* (Edinburgh: Banner of Truth, 1973), 368.

It becometh us to suffer ourselves to be taught in his name, and [to understand] that although the word which is preached unto us proceed out of the mouth of men, yet notwithstanding it is by the authority of God, and our salvation must be grounded thereupon, as well *as though heaven opened an hundred thousand times to show us the glory of God.*[20]

Have we God's word? At leastwise have we it preached purely? *Then is Jesus Christ as it were in the midst of us, and showeth himself as it were hanging upon the Cross,* witnessing what he did for us, when he suffered death to reconcile us to God his Father.[21]

When Calvin says here "as though" or "as it were," he is not implying that God is not really present. He is acknowledging that God is not *physically* audible or visible. It is "*as though* . . . we see him personally before us*" even though we do not see him personally. Instead of being physically present, God is *spiritually* present through the Word. Calvin describes the communication of Christ through his Word as "mystical," "incomprehensible," and "spiritual."[22]

The external minister administers the vocal word. . . . But the internal minister, who is the Holy Spirit, freely works internally, while by his secret virtue he effects in the hearts of whomsoever he will their union with Christ through one faith. This union is a thing internal, heavenly and indestructible.[23]

---

20. John Calvin, sermon on Gal. 1:1–5, in *Sermons on Galatians by John Calvin* (Audubon, NJ: Old Paths, 1995), 601–2.

21. John Calvin, sermon on Gal. 3:1–3, in *Sermons on Galatians by John Calvin*, 321.

22. John Calvin, "Summary of Doctrine concerning the Ministry of the Word and the Sacraments," in *Calvin: Theological Treatises*, ed. J. K. S. Reid, Library of Christian Classics 22 (Philadelphia: Westminster, 1954), 171–77.

23. Ibid., 173 (art. 5).

There is a parallel between preaching and the sacraments. In the sacraments we experience the presence of Christ through eating and drinking. Through preaching we experience the presence of Christ through speaking and listening. So preaching is not simply a word about Christ. It is "an offering and presentation of Christ."[24]

The Scriptures, the Spirit, and Faith

Like the sacraments, the Word of God does not work *ex opere operato*. This Latin phrase summarized the Catholic position on the effectiveness of the sacraments. It means "from the work worked." They believed that the sacraments worked by themselves, irrespective of the faith of those participating. The Reformers, as we shall see, believed that the sacraments are a promise or pledge to encourage our faith. In the same way, Calvin says of the Scriptures:

> We must hold that this efficacy is not contained in the words themselves, but proceeds from the secret instinct of the Spirit. . . . We hold, therefore, that when God speaks, he adds the efficacy of his Spirit, since his word without it would be fruitless.[25]

In other words, the Scriptures have value for us—when we respond with faith, they mediate the presence and comfort of Christ. So God sends the Spirit to awaken and strengthen faith when the Scriptures are preached. When people do not respond with faith, the Word is still effective, but its effect is to harden people for judgment.

Calvin begins the *Institutes* by stating that the two main objects of knowledge are God and humanity. Without knowledge

---

24. *Luther's Works*, 39:183.
25. Calvin, *Commentary*, on Ezek. 2:2. See also *Commentary*, on Acts 14:27.

of self there is no knowledge of God. His point is that true knowledge of God is relational. We know God as we know ourselves in relation to God. The more we see the perfections of God, the more we recognize our weaknesses. In some ways Calvin anticipates modern concerns about the relationship between subjective experience and objective reality. The two are linked because God has made us and then remade us to know him.

But Calvin also takes our fallenness seriously. This not only affects our ability to *obey* God. It also affects our ability to *know* God. Natural revelation does not lead to natural theology, because we reject the truth about God (Rom. 1:18–25). Our knowledge of God is distorted and corrupted by sin. As a result, we need Scripture. But Scripture is not enough, because we reject the truth in our sin. So we also need the regenerating work of the Holy Spirit. This means we cannot defend Scripture merely by using rational arguments, for the unbeliever deftly avoids their force. People also need the inner testimony of the Spirit. We use our natural faculties to understand Scripture, for its meaning is clear rather than coded. But the Spirit authenticates this to us as God's Word. The result is a grace-centered, Trinitarian hermeneutic. It is grace-centered because we cannot work it out for ourselves. We need God's help. It is Trinitarian because the Father testifies to his Son through the Spirit. And like the Trinity, the three cannot be separated. "By a kind of mutual bond" Word and Spirit are "joined together":

> For by a kind of mutual bond the Lord has joined together the certainty of his Word and of his Spirit so that the perfect religion of the Word may abide in our minds when the Spirit, who causes us to contemplate God's face, shines. . . . [God] sent down the same Spirit by whose power he had

dispensed the Word, to complete his work by the efficacious confirmation of the Word.[26]

This means we need both the external gift of the Word and the internal gift of faith through the Spirit. Calvin says that the relationship between preaching and faith is like a mother and her baby: "Preaching is the mother who conceives and brings forth, and faith is the daughter who ought to be mindful of her origin."[27] "Take away the preaching of the Gospel," he says, "and no faith will remain."[28]

Preaching and Preachers

So God is present when the Bible is read. Even more, he is present when the Word of God is preached in the gathering of the church. Luther says that the Word merely read "is not as fruitful and powerful as it is through a public preacher whom God has ordained to say and preach this."[29] And Calvin says:

> Those who neglect this means and yet hope to become perfect in Christ are mad. Such are the fanatics, who invent secret revelations of the Spirit for themselves, and the proud, who think that for them the private reading of the Scriptures is enough, and that they have no need of the common ministry of the Church.[30]

We know this in our experience. God does speak to us when we read our Bibles on our own. But more often and more

---

26. Calvin, *Institutes*, 1.9.3.
27. Calvin, *Commentary*, on 2 Cor. 13:5.
28. Calvin, *Commentary*, on Acts 16:31–32. See also *Commentary*, on 1 Cor. 3:6.
29. Martin Luther, sermon of July 21, 1532, in Jaroslav Pelikan, "Luther the Expositor," in *Luther's Works*, companion volume (St. Louis: Concordia, 1959), 64n66, cited in J. Mark Beach, "The Real Presence of Christ in the Preaching of the Gospel: Luther and Calvin on the Nature of Preaching," *Mid-America Journal of Theology* 10 (1999): 81.
30. Calvin, *Commentary*, on Eph. 4:12.

powerfully he speaks to us through the preaching of his Word when the church gathers under that Word.

The preaching of the Word conveys the voice and presence of Christ. This is clearly a high view of *preaching*. But Luther is careful not to make this a high view of *preachers*:

> When you hear a sermon by St. Paul or by me, you hear God the Father Himself. And yet you do not become my pupil but the Father's, for it is not I who is speaking; it is the Father. Nor am I your schoolmaster; but we both, you and I, have one Schoolmaster and Teacher, the Father, who instructs us. We both, pastor and listener, are only pupils; there is only this difference, that God is speaking to you through me. That is the glorious power of the divine Word, through which God Himself deals with us and speaks to us, and in which we hear God Himself.[31]

Luther loved to remind people of Balaam's donkey. In the story, God opens the mouth of the donkey so it can speak to Balaam (Numbers 22). Luther's argument is that if God can speak to Balaam through an ass, then God can speak to you through a human preacher.[32]

This high view of preaching obviously puts a great deal of responsibility on preachers. Luther says:

> Whoever, therefore, does not know or preach the gospel is not only no priest or bishop, but he is a kind of pest to the church, who under the false title of priest or bishop, or dressed in sheep's clothing, actually does violence to the gospel and plays the wolf [Matt. 7:15] in the church.[33]

---

31. Martin Luther, "Sermons on the Gospel of St. John," in *Luther's Works*, 23:97–98.
32. Ibid.
33. Martin Luther, *The Babylonian Captivity of the Church*, in *Luther's Works*, 36:116.

Preaching is a human act. As such, it is a fallible act. Preaching is not the word of God in the same way that the Bible is the word of God. Preaching is an *administration* of God's Word. It is an extension or application of God's revelation in Jesus testified in Scripture, rather than a second or rival source of revelation. So all preaching must be weighed according to the standard of God's infallible word in the Bible.

Nevertheless, God has chosen to use human preaching to convey his presence.

Come to the Preaching of God's Word to Hear Christ's Voice

Consider how this view would transform your attitude toward the preaching of your church each time you gather. Most of the time preaching feels very ordinary. As Luther says, all we hear is the voice of the preacher and all we see is a man. But God himself is addressing us. And he is addressing us to dispense the word of eternal life.

All sides of the church need to rediscover Christ present through his Word. Many Christians think of preaching as primarily a process of education. We come together to learn what the Bible teaches. This, of course, is true. Good preaching must involve teaching the Bible. Our authority comes from God's Word, so that Word needs to be understood.

But for the Reformers preaching was more than simply the transfer of information. The reality is that most of the time most of the congregation know the truths contained in the sermon. If you view preaching as simply a process of education, then you will tend to pursue novelty, and that is a dangerous path to pursue. Instead we come to the preaching of the Word as those who need to hear Christ's voice and encounter his presence. We need to hear from him words of reassurance or words of challenge. Sometimes we will learn new things. But this is not the measure of good preaching. A wife does not want new information on her wedding anniversary. She wants her husband to reassure her of his continuing love. This is what Christ does for his bride each week through the preaching of the Word.

COME TO THE PREACHING OF GOD'S
WORD WITH BLEEDING FEET

Consider these words from Calvin:

> There is nothing that should stir us up to embrace the teaching of the Gospel more than to learn that the pre-eminent worship of God, the sacrifice of a sweet odour, is to hear Him speaking by the mouth of men and to submit ourselves to *His Word as it is brought by men no less than if He himself had come down from heaven or had revealed His purpose by an angel.* And secondly, trust is confirmed and doubting removed when we hear that the witness to *our salvation is no less when declared by men sent of God than if His voice sounded from heaven.* On the other hand, to warn us of contempt of the Gospel, He adds the strong threat that those who refuse to hear ministers, however humble, are not insulting men but Himself and God the Father.[34]

Here is the irony. Many people today are desperate to hear the voice of God. They become obsessed with prophecies, dreams, and words of knowledge. Views of the ongoing role of prophecy differ. Some believe it has been superseded by the canon of Scripture. Others believe it is the Spirit-enabled application of Scripture to specific situations—something that

---

34. Calvin, *Commentary*, on Luke 10:16 (emphases added).

sometimes takes place in pastoral situations and often takes place in preaching.

But many people are not content with a Spirit-enabled application of Scripture. They want something extra. They want a direct communication from God. They are desperate to hear the voice of God. Yet week by week God is speaking to them in the preaching of the church. What we need to do is, as Luther puts it, "gradually train our hearts to believe that the preacher's words are God's Word."[35] Luther goes on: "People generally think: 'If I had an opportunity to hear God speak in person, I would run my feet bloody.' . . . But you now have the Word of God in church . . . and this is God's Word as surely as if God Himself were speaking to you."[36]

The real problem, I suspect, is that often people do not like what they hear through God's Word, read and preached. They want a word that allows them to circumvent the call to take up their cross daily. They want a word that justifies their desire for self-fulfillment or their sense of self-importance.

Why Scripture Still Matters

The challenge of the rule of Christ in his Word is both different from and similar to the challenges faced at the time of the Reformation. During the Reformation the main alternative to revelation was tradition. Today we perhaps suffer from a deficiency of tradition rather than a surfeit of it! What has replaced tradition as the rival to revelation is experience.

We have seen a dramatic loss of authority in the modern world. Now preference and experience are everything. Ethical issues are decided on the basis of the personal stories that elicit most sympathy. Individual dilemmas are determined on

35. Luther, "Sermons on the Gospel of St. John," in *Luther's Works*, 22:526–27.
36. Ibid.

the basis of a person's feelings. Any sense that right and wrong may be rooted in metaphysics (the way things are) or in divine revelation has been replaced by subjectivity.

We in the church are not immune to this cultural trend. Plenty of Christians believe the Bible is true. But the Reformers did not simply believe the Bible was true. We need to hear afresh the Reformation challenge of Scripture *alone*. Scripture alone is our supreme authority. The Bible is not just true; it is *truer* than anything else. So the Bible always trumps experience. That does not mean we must ignore experience. Experience will often give rise to questions we bring to Scripture. But Christ still reigns through his Word, read and preached. So we need to work hard to ensure that our lives and our life together are ruled not by tradition or experience, but by Christ through his Word.

3

Sin

What Is Wrong with Us?

Martin Luther grew up with a little view of sin. It was not that he refused to take sin seriously; quite the opposite. Sin, he was taught, is the foul smell that attracts the Devil; it is the weight that would drag us to hell; it is the cause of all misery, and its wages are death. Yet, while he knew it was a *severe* problem, he did not think it a very *deep* one.

It was a view that chimes well with today's cheery optimism about ourselves. Today we all know that we do some wrong things, but the suggestion that we may be rotten deep down strikes us as utterly repellent nonsense. There are a few wild-eyed baddies out there, we concede, but most of us are good people muddling our way through, and of course we slip up every now and again. What Luther came to see, surprisingly, was that such sunny stories of how basically good we are, so attractive in their cheeriness, are actually terrible, enslaving lies.

"Lies?" I hear the world scream. "How on earth can that be?" Well, the issue is simply this: if our problem is so small, it must be really easy to fix. My tendency to selfishness, to *use* others (including God) for my own ends, must be something *I* can sort out. Give me the right program and I will be able to root out all my failures; give me enough time and I may even sort myself out completely. It is the familiar message of the self-help program today, and it was the message Martin Luther was raised on.

In Luther's day it was the ancient Greek philosopher Aristotle who summed up the situation and whose message was so widespread: "We become righteous by doing righteous deeds," he had claimed (or "we become just by doing just acts").[1] It was a self-help, fake-it-till-you-make-it message. If you work at outward righteous acts and keep doing them, it claimed, you will actually become a righteous person.

Let me illustrate. Let us imagine that I have a friend we can call Tim. And let us say that this entirely fictional character has one serious character flaw that I have patiently put up with as his friend: he *hates* grannies. Whenever he sees a granny, a strange ache wells up in him to shove her under the nearest passing juggernaut. Now, as his friend, of course I want to help him. Here is the advice I would have to give him if I were to use the Aristotle method: "Tim," I would say, "you become a granny-lover by granny-loving deeds, so if you'll help ten grannies *safely* cross the road every day for one month, then you'll be rid of that rather unsociable phobia of yours." Of course, it would be risky advice to give Tim: so much contact with sweet senior citizens might simply aggravate his condition.

---

1. Aristotle, *The Nicomachean Ethics*, trans. and intro. D. Ross, rev. J. L. Ackrill and J. O. Urmson (Oxford: Oxford University Press, 1998), 29.

In fact that was just how Luther found it (though without the grannies). For years he lived by the maxim "We become righteous by doing righteous deeds." As a monk he desperately did all the righteous deeds he could imagine: fasting, praying, pilgrimages, and monkery. What he slowly came to realize was that the dream of becoming truly righteous by such a simple change of behavior was just that: an elusive dream. Holding its reward ever just out of reach, it constantly promised righteousness without delivering it, all the time exacting a heavier and heavier behavioral demand.

In other words, by dangling the hope of being righteous before him while repeatedly giving more deeds to do, it gradually enslaved him. Not only was doing all the outward acts of righteousness not making him upright in heart; it was making things worse. He found in himself resentment snowballing against the God who demands so many deeds. Trying to sort himself out and become righteous by his own efforts was driving him deep down into slavery, despair, and hatred of God. Sin, he began to see, was not so easy a problem to whisk away. It went deep down, deeper than he could reach by himself.

High Noon

So it was, in 1517, that Luther decided to challenge Aristotle. A few weeks before posting his famous ninety-five theses, he penned his ninety-seven theses, in which he wrote:

> We do *not* become righteous by doing righteous deeds but, *having been made righteous*, we do righteous deeds. . . .
>
> It is an error to say that no man can become a theologian without Aristotle. . . .
>
> Indeed, no one can become a theologian unless he becomes one without Aristotle. . . .

Briefly, the whole Aristotle is to theology as darkness is to light.[2]

That is, our sin is not something we can sort out by ourselves by adjusting our performance. If we are to be righteous, we have to be *made* righteous. So how does that work? Luther continues:

> The grace of God, however, makes righteousness abound through Jesus Christ because it causes one to be pleased with the law.
>
> Every deed of the law without the grace of God appears good outwardly, but inwardly it is sin. . . .
>
> The good law and that in which one lives is the love of God, spread abroad in our hearts by the Holy Spirit.[3]

What we cannot do, the grace of God does. For God in his kindness is able to reach down where we cannot reach and change not just the superficial layer of our behavior, but our very hearts, causing us actually to *desire* ("to be pleased with") what is righteous. And that uprightness of the heart is the only true uprightness.

The Question on Which Everything Hinges

This is just where many would part ways with the Reformation: God's saving people out of his sheer loving-kindness sounds wonderful; but people *needing* to be saved because they are otherwise helpless in their sin sounds less pleasing. And we do not like hearing bad news.

It was the same in Luther's day. In the early days of the Reformation there were many—especially among those who had been drawn to the Renaissance—who were broadly, if only

---

2. *Luther's Works*, 31:12 (emphasis added).
3. *Luther's Works*, 31:14–15.

vaguely, sympathetic to the Reformation. They saw the need for some sort of reformation in the church, they wanted the corruption and mismanagement cleaned up, and men like Luther seemed to them to be stepping up to the task. One such admirer was Erasmus, at the time the most celebrated scholar in the world and the man who had published the Greek New Testament that had converted Luther. Yet Erasmus's idea of reformation was like his view of Christianity: he believed that what the Roman Catholic Church needed in his day was a few improvements. It was dirty and needed a wash, but nothing more radical or essential needed changing. Likewise, we all, he felt, could and should do better, but that does not at all mean that we are *enslaved* to our sin.

So in 1524 Erasmus wrote *On the Freedom of the Will*, arguing that sin is *not* something that affects us so deeply or powerfully that it actually enslaves us. We can never earn *true* merit before God, Erasmus admitted, but God *is* prepared to take our good intentions and so treat our attempts as better than they really are and so worthy of merit. It is as if God takes the molehills of our righteousness and treats them as mountains. But if Luther was right that in ourselves we can produce *no* righteousness to count toward our salvation, what credit can anyone have with God? With this argument Erasmus seems to have entirely missed Luther's answer, that we who have no righteousness of our own can have the righteousness of Christ credited to us.

Erasmus saw *On the Freedom of the Will* as a gentle, scholarly correction of an overstatement by a hot-headed young Reformer. Luther did not usually bother with arguments against his theology (there were simply too many), but this he saw as an assault on the very vitals of the Reformation, and he replied with a blistering argument, *On the Bondage of the Will.* "Now, my good Erasmus," he wrote,

> you alone have attacked the real issue, the essence of the matter in dispute, and have not wearied me with irrelevancies about the papacy, purgatory, indulgences, and such like trifles (for trifles they are rather than basic issues), with which almost everyone hitherto has gone hunting for me without success. You and you alone have seen the question on which everything hinges, and have aimed at the vital spot; for which I sincerely thank you.[4]

The title Luther gave his work, *On the Bondage of the Will,* commonly throws people. "I make free choices, don't I? Is Luther saying that I can't do what I want?" they ask. "But that's complete nonsense: I do what I want every day! My will seems very free." Actually, Luther would agree: we *do* always do what we want. We freely choose to do the things we do, and in that sense our wills are entirely free. However, you do not choose what to want. For underneath our wills, directing and governing our choices, lie our hearts with all their inclinations and desires. "The *heart* of man plans his way" (Prov. 16:9). When faced with even the most basic choice—say a bacon cheeseburger versus a plate of celery—you will find yourself *wanting* one and not the other. Your choice will be determined by your desire. And those who choose the celery over the burger do not negate the rule: they choose it because they desire to be vegetarian, because they have a tragic intolerance and desire not to be ill, or because the desire to be healthy has trumped the desire for immediate deliciousness.

That is why we choose to sin. It is not because we are forced into it: "When a man is without the Spirit of God he does not

---

4. *Luther's Works*, 33:294.

do evil against his will, as if he were taken by the scruff of the neck and forced to it."⁵ But nor is it because we neutrally weigh the odds of each decision and choose what seems most sensible. It is because we are "carrying out the *desires* of the body" (Eph. 2:3). We choose sin because that is what we want. We naturally *love* darkness (John 3:19), and so "each person is tempted when he is lured and enticed *by his own desire*. Then desire when it has conceived gives birth to sin, and sin when it is fully grown brings forth death" (James 1:14–15).

The Radicality of Our Problem

What Luther saw was that the problem of our sin goes as deep in us as it possibly can: all the way down into our hearts, shaping what we want and love. As a result, we never naturally want God. We freely choose to do the things we want—and that may include living a life of outward morality and respectability—but left to ourselves we shall never choose God, because we do not naturally want him.

Erasmus took it that our problem as sinners is basically sloth. We are spiritually sluggish and sleepy, and what we need if we are to be righteous is to pull ourselves together and put in the proper effort. But Luther's own experience gave the lie to that: all his extraordinary religious effort left him sighing, "I did not love, yes, I hated the righteous God who punishes sinners, and secretly, if not blasphemously, certainly murmuring greatly, I was angry with God."⁶ With that in his heart, he could strive as hard as he wanted and yet find himself only further than ever from actually fulfilling the law by loving the Lord his God. An outward *appearance* of righteousness he could achieve, but

---

5. *Luther's Works*, 33:64.
6. *Luther's Works*, 34:336–37.

it would be nothing more than a hollow sham made of self-dependence, self-worship, and self-righteousness.

He was like a rotten tree producing rotten fruit, his religious efforts no more than attempts to staple plastic fakes on his branches to disguise the problem. Sin was in his roots, in the very grain of his deepest self. Nothing was unscathed by it or neutral. What Luther needed—and what he came to see all sinners need—was a *radical* renewal: a new heart that would freely love and be pleased with God (Ezek. 36:26–27; Mark 7:14–23; John 3:3). And that would come about only through "the love of God, spread abroad in our hearts by the Holy Spirit" (Rom. 5:5).[7] As he would later put it, "the heart must be made glad. . . . The heart must grow warm and melt in the love of God. *Then* praise and thanksgiving will follow with a pure heart."[8] It is when people taste the love, grace, and glory of God through the gospel that their eyes are opened and their hearts turned: only then will they love God back with a pure heart.

Two Different Visions

The difference between Luther and Erasmus as they debated how deep sin goes could look rather specialist and obscure. That, in fact, was just how Erasmus saw it. However, their differences at this point meant that Luther and Erasmus ended up with two quite different visions of Christianity.

For Erasmus the church was most like an army (one of his best-known works was entitled *The Manual of the Christian Soldier*). The important thing, then, for a Christian, was to keep the rules and do one's duty. This does not mean that Erasmus was concerned only about the externals of religion. Far from it. Witness this advice from *The Manual*:

---

7. *Luther's Works*, 31:14–15.
8. *Luther's Works*, 44:56 (emphasis added).

Of what use is it to be sprinkled on the outside by holy water if filthy within? . . . No devotion better pleases Mary than the imitation of her humility. . . . Would you please Peter and Paul? Then emulate the faith of the one and the charity of the other. Thereby you will do better than if you make ten pilgrimages to Rome. Would you imitate St. Francis? As it is you are arrogant, avaricious, and contentious. Control your temper, despise lucre. Overcome evil with good.[9]

Erasmus urges his readers to be humbler, more charitable, self-controlled, and so on. But that is not necessarily the same thing as knowing and loving God. Behavior and character were what mattered for Erasmus: a relationship with God does not feature in his twenty-two rules for the Christian soldier.

For Luther, on the other hand, the church is more like a family. *Knowing* God the Father is what matters above all. Sin is not just substandard behavior and a dereliction of proper duty: *to sin is to despise God*. The act of sin has its roots in the heart and reveals that something other than God has become the true object of the heart's desire and adoration. Likewise, Christian life is not primarily about acting humbly or charitably: such things are the *consequences* of being truly alive. According to Jesus, "*this* is eternal life, that they know you the only true God, and Jesus Christ whom you have sent" (John 17:3).

When those two visions are played out in real life, the difference between them becomes even more obvious. If right behavior is the goal, and if that is a goal all people can achieve by simply exerting themselves properly, then the church *can* run just like an army. Pastors can serve as the sergeant majors,

---

9. Desiderius Erasmus, *The Enchiridion*, trans. Raymond Himelick (Bloomington: Indiana University Press, 1965), 124.

drilling their troops into line. After all, for Erasmus everyone is *capable* of getting into line.

But if we were made for a deeper purpose—to love, glorify, and enjoy God[10]—and yet we *cannot* naturally love him, being enslaved to sin, then merely to order people to do what they cannot would be cruel. In other words, anyone who comes to hold Luther's deep view of sin must find his or her compassion swell. For people are not just naturally lazy; they are helpless. They need their very hearts to be dealt with, not simply their performance. Above all, they need the one thing with the power to turn and liberate their hearts: the gospel (Rom. 1:16). "How shall a work please God if it proceeds from a reluctant and resisting heart?" asked Luther.

> To fulfil the law, however, is to do its works with pleasure and love. . . . This pleasure and love for the law is put into the heart by the Holy Spirit. . . . But the Holy Spirit is not given except in, with, and by faith in Jesus Christ. . . . Faith, moreover, comes only through God's Word or gospel, which preaches Christ.[11]

If hearts that are enslaved to the charming lies of sin are ever to be won to God, the glory of God in the face of Christ must be made known to them. He must be shown to be *better*, more desirable than our sin. And that was how Luther would minister to people. Compare, then, Erasmus's stern counsel with this from Luther:

> I could not have faith in God if I did not think he wanted to be favorable and kind to me. This in turn makes me feel

---

10. Neatly distilling just over a century of Reformation theology, the first question of the Westminster Shorter Catechism (1647) asks, "What is the chief end of man? *Answer:* Man's chief end is to glorify God, and to enjoy him forever."

11. *Luther's Works*, 35:368.

kindly disposed toward him, and I am moved to trust him with all my heart and to look to him for all good things. . . . Look here! This is how you must cultivate Christ in yourself. . . . Faith must spring up and flow from the blood and wounds and death of Christ. If you see in these that God is so kindly disposed toward you that he even gives his own Son for you, then your heart in turn must grow sweet and disposed toward God. . . . We never read that the Holy Spirit was given to anybody because he had performed some works, but always when men have heard the gospel of Christ and the mercy of God.[12]

Because sin is a slavery or addiction, Luther saw that he could not simply hector or order people out of it. That might bring about behavior change, but it would only reinforce a deeper self-dependence. Ears need to be opened to the message of Christ and him crucified so that eyes can open to the unfathomable kindness and glory of the living God. Only in that gospel light can true humility, goodness, and charity grow.

Pressing Home the Point

People do not easily abandon the idea that sin is but a cosmetic problem, so Luther deployed one more line of reasoning to help convince us. As well as making a case for *how deep* sin goes in us, he also sought to clarify *what* sin is. Our trouble, he believed, is that we do not actually know what sin is. Why? Because we do not know the God whom sin offends. We are ignorant of our sin because of our sin. Curved in on ourselves, we fail to see ourselves—or our problem—aright. For all our self-obsessed struggle to better ourselves, we fail to recognize our most basic failure: we do not love and trust God (Rom.

---

12. *Luther's Works*, 44:30, 38–39.

14:23). We are bent in on ourselves because we have turned away from God.

This left Luther with a definition of sin that brought condemnation crashing down even on those who felt they were keeping Erasmus's twenty-two rules for the Christian soldier. You could imitate Mary's humility and emulate St. Francis's self-control, but still you would be guilty of the worst sin. "The worst sin is not to accept the Word."[13] No attempt to improve my character or behavior could undo that fundamental sin against the first commandment. In fact all such attempts would only compound the sin by the arrogant assumption that, like God, I can produce righteousness and eternal life for myself. For

> what greater contempt of God is there than not believing his promise? For what is this but to make God a liar or to doubt that he is truthful?—that is, to ascribe truthfulness to one's self but lying and vanity to God? Does not a man who does this deny God and set himself up as an idol in his heart?[14]

Not everyone on the side of the Reformation saw the issue with Luther's clarity. The Zurich Reformer Huldrych Zwingli focused on idolatry as the problem of the day: people trusting in relics and saints instead of God. For Luther, though, idolatry was consequential, failure to keep the second commandment flowing from a failure to keep the first. The reason people were turning to idols was that in their hearts they had already turned from God. Even before being guilty of idolatry they were guilty of contempt of God. Idolatry, contempt of neighbor, and ingratitude were just symptoms of the underlying sickness.

---

13. *Luther's Works*, 17:383.
14. *Luther's Works*, 31:350.

The Ugly Duckling

The Reformation's "deep" view of sin is rather like the proverbial ugly duckling: initially unattractive and embarrassing, but secretly a thing of promise. It is a doctrine of promise because without it Christ is robbed of his saving glory, and the gospel loses its wonder. If sin is not much of a problem, Christ need not be much of a Savior, and we do not need much grace.

Only if I see my plight is so bad that I cannot fix it myself will I find true freedom in Christ, for only then will I stop depending on myself and depend on him. Only then will I despair of my own efforts and look outside myself for hope. This is just what we see in the Gospels: it is the one with the great debt canceled who loves his old creditor most (Luke 7:40–43); it is the forgiven prostitutes and tax collectors who weep with joy, give away their wealth, and love Jesus. It is the Pharisees—those who think they have something in themselves on which to depend—who never find that liberation and transformation.

Historically, too, times of church reformation and revival have consistently been marked by a radical view of sin. It was on the lips of the preachers of the Great Awakening—men like George Whitefield and Jonathan Edwards—as much as it was in the mouths of the Reformers. Such men knew that calls for social improvement and better morality, while good things, never touch the depths of the human condition. Corrupted all the way down, we cannot fix ourselves. Our hearts must be renewed, and that can happen only through the gospel being preached and the glory of God being unveiled.

The Reformation's radical view of sin is *why* we sinners must throw ourselves on God's grace alone.

4

Grace

What Does God Give Us?

Years before the Reformation, in his days as a monk, Martin Luther had begun lecturing on the Bible at the university in Wittenberg. There he taught his students that salvation is by grace. "Not because of our merits," he explained; salvation is "given out of the pure mercy of the promising God."[1] No alarms went off; not a single eyebrow was raised among all the inquisitors in Rome. And why not? Because Martin Luther the monk was still then upholding Rome's own theology. He was loyally teaching standard medieval Roman Catholicism, that salvation is by *grace*.

Eyebrows might not have arched in Rome, but perhaps yours did just then. For was not the whole point of the Reformation that medieval Roman Catholicism falsely taught salvation by

---

1. *Luther's Works*, 11:396–97.

works? That, certainly, is how many see it. Yet that idea actually fails to grasp how things really were. More importantly, it fails to grasp the true wonder and acuteness of the Reformers' message.

Grace in Medieval Roman Catholicism

What, then, did Luther the monk (before the Reformation) mean when he taught salvation by grace? He could state that salvation "is not on the basis of our merits but on the pure promise of a merciful God." Which sounds all very Reformational—until he goes on to explain:

> Hence the teachers correctly say that *to a man who does what is in him* God gives grace without fail. . . . [God] bestows everything gratis and only on the basis of the promise of his mercy, *although he wants us to be prepared for this as much as lies in us.*[2]

So, according to this, God *does* save by grace, *but* that grace is given to those who are "prepared" for it, who do "what is in them" to be fit for grace. Or as others ("the teachers") of the day liked to put it, "God will not deny grace to those who do their best."

Romans 5:5 is perhaps the single most helpful verse for understanding this view of salvation by grace. "God's love has been poured into our hearts through the Holy Spirit who has been given to us," writes the apostle Paul. Instead of being read as a verse about the transformative work of the Spirit in those who "*have been* justified by faith" (Rom. 5:1), as the context proves, Romans 5:5 was taken as an account of salvation, meaning that God pours his love and grace into our hearts,

---

2. *Luther's Works*, 11:396–97 (emphases added).

transforming us and making us holy—holy enough, ultimately, for heaven.

Our problem, according to this theology, is that, while God is holy, we are spiritually lazy. Only holy people belong with a holy God in heaven, but, while we may recognize the problem, we really cannot be bothered. We do not seem able to summon up the energy needed to be truly holy. And so God in his kindness gives us *grace*. As we saw earlier, grace is thus a bit like a can of spiritual Red Bull. I find myself unable to pull myself together and get holy. Then God gives me grace, and suddenly I find myself much more eager and able.

This, then, *was* a theology of salvation by grace: without this grace, we could never become the sort of holy people it claimed belong in heaven. But it was absolutely *not* a theology of salvation by grace *alone*. Here grace provided the necessary boost this theology imagined we all need to earn eternal life; but it did not actually give or guarantee eternal life itself. The Red Bull of grace would be given to those who wanted and pursued it, and it saved only insofar as it *enabled* people to become holy and so win their salvation.

This might all have been the theology of sixteenth-century Roman Catholicism, but it does not feel too unfamiliar to twenty-first-century Protestants and evangelicals. "Grace" is still routinely thought of today as a package of blessing doled out by God. And, small details aside, that picture captures well a common and instinctive view of salvation: that while we know God saves by grace, we still look to ourselves and our performance to know how we stand before him. Our prayer lives are often painfully revealing of this. Every day Christians *should* be able to approach the Almighty and boldly cry, "Our Father," *all because of Jesus*. As we read in Hebrews, "Since then we have a great high priest who has passed through the heavens, Jesus, the Son of God. . . . Let us then with confidence draw near to the throne of grace" (Heb. 4:14–16). Yet in practice our sins and failings make us shrink back. Ignoring Jesus's salvation, we feel we cannot approach the Holy One *because of how we have performed.*

Having tasted the bitter dregs of this self-dependent theology, Luther wrote:

> It's true. I was a good monk and kept my order so strictly that I could say that if ever a monk could get to heaven through monastic discipline, I should have entered in. All my companions in the monastery who knew me would bear me out in this. For if it had gone on much longer, I would have martyred myself to death, what with vigils, prayers, readings, and other works. . . . And yet my conscience would not give me certainty, but I always doubted and said, "You didn't do that right. You weren't contrite enough. You left that out of your confession." The more I tried to remedy an uncertain, weak and troubled conscience with human traditions, the more daily I found it more uncertain, weaker and more troubled.[3]

Grace in the Reformation

Luther's Reformation message of salvation by grace *alone* could hardly have looked more different when compared with that old pre-Reformation teaching of his about salvation by grace. This is how he began to talk: "He is not righteous who does much, but he who, without work, believes much in Christ."[4] Here grace is not about God's building on our righteous deeds or helping us to perform them. God, Luther began to see, was

---

3. *D. Martin Luthers Werke: Kritische Gesamtausgabe*, 127 vols. (Weimar: Böhlau, 1883–2009), 38:143, cited in Alister E. McGrath, *Reformation Thought: An Introduction* (Oxford: Blackwell, 1988), 72.
4. Thesis 25, Heidelberg Disputation, in *Luther's Works*, 31:55.

the one "who justifies the *un*godly" (Rom. 4:5), not one who simply recognizes and rewards those who manage to make themselves godly. God is not one who must build on our foundations; he creates life out of *nothing*. It meant that, instead of looking to God for assistance and then ultimately relying on himself, Luther was turning to rely *entirely* on Christ, in whom all righteousness is achieved. "The law says, 'do this,' and it is never done. Grace says, 'believe in this,' and *everything is already done*."[5]

Here Luther found a message so good it almost seemed incredible to him. It was good news for the repeated failure, news of a God who comes not to call the righteous but sinners (Matt. 9:13). Not many today find themselves wearing hair shirts and enduring all-night prayer vigils in the freezing cold to earn God's favor. Yet deep in our psyche is the assumption that we *will* be more loved when (and only when) we make ourselves more attractive—both to God and to others. Into that, Luther speaks words that cut through the gloom like a glorious and utterly unexpected sunbeam:

> The love of God does not find, but creates, that which is pleasing to it. . . . Rather than seeking its own good, the love of God flows forth and bestows good. Therefore sinners are attractive because they are loved; they are not loved because they are attractive.[6]

In Reformation thought, grace was no longer seen as being like a can of spiritual Red Bull. It was more like a marriage. In fact when Luther first sought to explain his Reformation discovery in detail to the world, it was the story of a wedding that framed what he said. Drawing on the romance of the lover and

---

5. Thesis 26, *Luther's Works*, 31:56 (emphasis added).
6. Thesis 28, *Luther's Works*, 31:57.

his beloved in Song of Solomon (especially 2:16, "My beloved is mine, and I am his"), he told the gospel as the story of the "rich and divine bridegroom Christ" who "marries this poor, wicked harlot, redeems her from all her evil, and adorns her with all his goodness."[7] At the wedding a wonderful exchange takes place whereby the king takes all the shame and debt of his bride, and the harlot receives all the wealth and royal status of her bridegroom. For Jesus and the soul that is united to him by faith, it works like this:

> Christ is full of grace, life, and salvation. The soul is full of sins, death, and damnation. Now let faith come between them and sins, death, and damnation will be Christ's, while grace, life, and salvation will be the soul's; for if Christ is a bridegroom, he must take upon himself the things which are his bride's and bestow upon her the things that are his. If he gives her his body and very self, how shall he not give her all that is his? And if he takes the body of the bride, how shall he not take all that is hers?[8]

In the story the prostitute finds that she has been made a queen. That does not mean she always *behaves* as befits royalty but, however she behaves, her *status* is royal. She *is* now the queen. So it is with the believer: she remains a sinner and continues to stumble and wander, but she has the righteous status of her perfect and royal bridegroom. She is—and until death will remain—at the same time both utterly righteous (in her status before God) and a sinner (in her behavior).

That means that it is simply wrong-headed for the believer to look to her behavior as an accurate yardstick of her righteousness before God. Her behavior and her status are distinct.

---

7. *Luther's Works*, 31:352.
8. *Luther's Works*, 31:351.

The prostitute will grow more queenly as she lives with the king and feels the security of his love, but she will never become *more* the queen. Just so, the believer will grow more Christlike over time, but never more righteous. Thus, because of Christ, and not because of her performance, the sinner can know a despair-crushing confidence.

> Her sins cannot now destroy her, since they are laid upon Christ and swallowed up by him. And she has that righteousness in Christ, her husband, of which she may boast as of her own and which she can confidently display alongside her sins in the face of death and hell and say, "If I have sinned, yet my Christ, in whom I believe, has not sinned, and all his is mine and all mine is his."[9]

For the rest of his life Luther took this message as good news that needs continually to be reapplied to the heart of the believer. From his own experience he found that we are so instinctively self-dependent that while we happily subscribe to salvation by grace, our minds are like rocks, drawn down by the gravitational pull of sin away from belief in grace *alone*. So he counseled his friend as follows:

> They try to do good of themselves in order that they might stand before God clothed in their own virtues and merits. But this is impossible. Among us you were one who held to this opinion, or rather, error. So was I, and *I am still fighting against the error without having conquered it as yet.*
>
> Therefore, my dear brother, learn Christ and him crucified. Learn to pray to him and, despairing of yourself, say: "Thou, Lord Jesus, art my righteousness, but I am thy sin. Thou hast taken upon thyself what is mine and hast given to

---

9. *Luther's Works*, 31:352.

me what is thine. Thou hast taken upon thyself what thou wast not and hast given to me what I was not."[10]

What Is Grace?

There is far more than first meets the eye standing between the Roman Catholic idea of salvation by grace and the Reformation's message of salvation by grace alone. The fact that just one little word ("alone") distinguishes them makes one feel that only the fussiest theologian could tell them apart. But the difference actually involves even more than where we should look for confidence before God: the very *meaning* of the word "grace" is quite different in each.

In Roman Catholicism grace was seen as a "thing," a force or fuel like Red Bull. Catholics would pray, "Hail, Mary, *full of grace*," as if Mary were wired with spiritual caffeine. Perhaps the clearest illustration of this concept of grace is seen in Father (later Cardinal) John Henry Newman's otherwise marvelous hymn "Praise to the Holiest in the Height":

> Praise to the Holiest in the height,
> And in the depth be praise;
> In all His words most wonderful,
> Most sure in all His ways.
>
> O loving wisdom of our God!
> When all was sin and shame,
> A second Adam to the fight
> And to the rescue came.
>
> O wisest love! that flesh and blood,
> Which did in Adam fail,

---

10. To George Spenlein, in *Luther: Letters of Spiritual Counsel*, ed. T. G. Tappert, Library of Christian Classics 18 (Vancouver: Regent College, 2003), 110 (emphasis added).

Should strive afresh against the foe,
Should strive and should prevail.

And that a higher gift than grace
Should flesh and blood refine,
God's Presence and His very Self,
And Essence all divine.

In Newman's mind "God's Presence and His very Self" is something *different* from "grace." Grace is a gift, but God's presence is a "*higher gift* than grace."

That is nothing like how Luther and his fellow Reformers saw grace. For them, grace was not a "thing" at all; it is the personal kindness of God by which he does not merely enable us but actually rescues and (note the contrast to Newman) freely gives us *himself*. Or, to be even more precise: there is no such "thing" as grace; there is only Christ, who is the blessing of God freely given to us. That being the case, Luther tended not to talk much about grace in the abstract, preferring to speak of Christ. For example:

> Therefore faith justifies because it takes hold of and possesses *this* treasure, the present Christ . . . the Christ who is grasped by faith and who lives in the heart is the true Christian righteousness, on account of which God counts us righteous and grants us eternal life.[11]

In other words, the grace and righteousness we receive in the gospel are not something other than Christ himself: "Christ . . . *is* the divine Power, Righteousness, Blessing, Grace, and Life."[12] Compare, then, Newman's hymn with this, by Luther:

---

11. *Luther's Works*, 26:130 (emphasis added).
12. *Luther's Works*, 26:282 (emphasis added).

Dear Christians, one and all, rejoice,
With exultation springing,
And with united heart and voice
And holy rapture singing,
Proclaim the wonders God has done,
How his right arm the victory won;
What price our ransom cost him!

To me he [Christ] spoke: "Cling fast to me,
I am your rock and castle.
Your ransom I myself will be;
For you I strive and wrestle.
For I am yours, and you are mine,
And where I am you may remain;
The foe shall not divide us."

For Luther, God does not give something other than himself; in his grace he unites us to his Son by his Spirit that we might share the life and righteousness of the Son. Instead of handing out some enabling blessing, Christ makes *himself* ours, and so totally that we may plead what is his as ours.

Living under Grace Alone

What difference does living under grace alone make? Clearly, anyone who can know that they are accepted and loved by God because of Jesus and not because of how well they have done can know a confidence as secure as Jesus himself. In him they have an unsurpassable righteousness that is, like him, "the same yesterday and today and forever" (Heb. 13:8).

But may it lead them to be perhaps a little *too* confident? With heaven in the bag, may they feel they can "continue in sin that grace may abound" (Rom. 6:1)? May they not argue that while they like sinning, God likes forgiving? That was just what many Roman Catholics wondered when they heard the Reformers' message. And ever since, it has not just been Roman Catholics who have seen the dangers. In the twentieth century, surrounded by a people—and a church—that had so easily capitulated to Hitler, the *Lutheran* pastor Dietrich Bonhoeffer felt that a wrong attitude toward grace was partly to blame. On the eve of the Second World War he wrote a scalding attack on what he called the "cheap grace" that had allowed such moral spinelessness:

> Cheap grace means the justification of sin without the justification of the sinner. Grace alone does everything, they say, and so everything can remain as it was before. "All for sin could not atone." The world goes on in the same old way, and we are still sinners "even in the best life" as Luther said. Well, then, let the Christian live like the rest of the world, let him model himself on the world's standards in every sphere of life, and not presumptuously aspire to live a different life under grace from his old life under sin. . . .
>
> Cheap grace is the preaching of forgiveness without requiring repentance. . . . Cheap grace is grace without discipleship, grace without the cross, *grace without Jesus Christ*, living and incarnate.[13]

Bonhoeffer's phrase "grace without Jesus Christ" is really the key here. For "grace without Jesus Christ" was precisely what the Reformers were stepping *away from*. With their message of grace alone they were not offering more of grace as "stuff" or spiritual fuel; they were offering Christ. In other words, salvation by *grace* alone is simply another way of saying salvation by *Christ* alone. "Through faith in Christ," wrote Luther, "Christ's righteousness becomes our righteousness and all

---

13. Dietrich Bonhoeffer, *The Cost of Discipleship* (London: SCM, 1948), 35–36 (emphasis added).

that he has becomes ours; *rather, He Himself becomes ours.*[14] And that puts a world of difference between the message of grace alone and cheap grace.

As Luther showed in his marriage illustration, salvation by grace alone is about the believer's being united to Christ as a bridegroom is united to his bride. In the story, the prostitute receives the royal status of her husband, but that does not tell us about the *point* or *intent* of the marriage. Marriages are supposed to point to the ideal marriage between Christ and the church (Eph. 5:31–32). And in an ideal marriage a man and a woman come together in order to get *each other*. Just so, believers trust in Christ and are united to him in order to get *him*. Not, first and foremost, to get heaven, righteousness, life, or any other blessing, but to get Christ, in whom all those other blessings are then found. Take the apostle Paul, who wrote so emphatically on salvation by grace alone. Writing to the Philippians he declared that his desire was to depart and be not "in heaven" but "with Christ" (Phil. 1:23). For him, Christ was the greatest attraction of heaven.

It all means that nobody can truly receive the Christ who justifies without receiving the Christ who makes us holy. The eternal life that believers freely receive by faith alone *is* the life of the Spirit, who transforms us so that we become ever holier and more Christlike (2 Cor. 3:18). That means that holy living is not the awkward small print of the gospel, a catch hiding behind the good news of grace alone. This is itself wonderful good news: through this gospel God acts to free us not only from the horrifying future penalty of sin, but also from its present enslaving power. Grace alone is the most potent message of liberation: total liberation from hell, and gradual liberation

---

14. *Luther's Works*, 31:298 (emphasis added).

even from its toxic but addictive foretastes. Thus Paul can write that

> *the grace of God* has appeared, bringing salvation for all people, *training us* to renounce ungodliness and worldly passions, and to live self-controlled, upright, and godly lives in the present age, waiting for our blessed hope, the appearing of the glory of our great God and Savior Jesus Christ, *who gave himself for us to redeem us from all lawlessness* and to purify for himself a people for his own possession who are zealous for good works. (Titus 2:11–14)

Because true grace is never "grace without Jesus Christ," Paul has no intellectual difficulty in putting "free salvation" right alongside "good works":

> For by grace you have been saved through faith. And this is not your own doing; it is the gift of God, not a result of works, so that no one may boast. *For* we are his workmanship, created in Christ Jesus for good works, which God prepared beforehand, that we should walk in them. (Eph. 2:8–10)

There is no difficulty here, for that is the only true life, and the life for which believers are freely saved: to be freed from the captivity of sin, to know God and to share his good and holy life.

My Chains Fell Off

There is a consistent testimony down through the centuries: those who have accepted that God saves by his grace alone have found the message to be one of unutterably sweet liberation. Martin Luther wrote that, on his discovery of it, "I felt that I was altogether born again and had entered paradise itself through open gates."[15] A few years later in England William Tyndale would call it "merry, glad and joyful tidings, that maketh a man's heart glad and maketh him sing, dance, and leap for joy."[16]

But two reactions to this message stand out as near identical, though almost a century separates them. The first is that of John Bunyan, the seventeenth-century author of *The Pilgrim's Progress*. On discovering that his righteousness was all to be found in Christ and not himself, he exclaimed, "*Now did my chains fall off my legs indeed*, I was loosed from my affliction and irons."[17] The second is that of Charles Wesley, the eighteenth-century hymnwriter. In his well-known hymn "And Can It Be?" he describes his discovery of the salvation that is "mercy all, immense and free":

Long my imprisoned spirit lay,
Fast bound in sin and nature's night;
Thine eye diffused a quickening ray—
I woke, the dungeon flamed with light;
My chains fell off, my heart was free,
I rose, went forth, and followed Thee.

No condemnation now I dread;
Jesus, and all in Him, is mine;
Alive in Him, my living Head,
And clothed in righteousness divine,
Bold I approach th'eternal throne,
And claim the crown, through Christ my own.

15. *Luther's Works*, 34:337.
16. William Tyndale, "A Pathway into the Holy Scripture," in *The Works of William Tyndale*, 2 vols. (Cambridge: Parker Society, 1848; repr., Edinburgh: Banner of Truth, 2010), 1:8.
17. John Bunyan, *Grace Abounding* (Oxford: Oxford University Press, 1998), 66.

For both Bunyan and Wesley the message of grace alone was a prison escape.

And so it remains today. The Reformers' tenacious insistence on grace *alone* is no relic of the history books to be looked on with embarrassment as the sorry squabble of persnickety theologians. It remains today as the only message of ultimate liberation, the message with the deepest power to make humans unfurl and flourish. For by grace alone all who know themselves as failures can know not just a bit of spiritual enabling from God, helping them do better; they can know a wholly new and victorious identity in Christ. They can know assurance, relief from guilt, and sweet intimacy with an almighty Father who cares for them. And, as Charles Wesley showed, knowing *that*, they begin to find a hearty desire rising up in them to follow the One who is the source of all grace and every good. Once they might have attempted holiness out of the desperate desire to earn eternal life; now they do so out of a heart transformed to want Christ and to see the beauty of his kindness, his goodness, his generosity, and all his holy ways.

5

The Theology of the Cross

How Do We Know What Is True?

As news of Martin Luther's protest against the Catholic Church began to spread, it created a big stink. Pope Leo X wanted Luther disciplined and gave the job to the Augustinian Order, since at this point Luther was still an Augustinian monk. The job fell to Johann von Staupitz, Luther's superior in the order. But instead of disciplining Luther, Staupitz invited him to present his ideas to the Augustinians for discussion.

The gathering took place on April 26, 1518, at Heidelberg. Luther produced forty-two theses for the occasion—the so-called Heidelberg Disputation. There were twenty-eight on theology. And because Luther was essentially attacking medieval theology, he also added fourteen theses attacking the scholastic interpretation of Aristotle. We have the forty-two theses, but we also have a record of Luther's explanations, so each thesis has an accompanying set of comments:[1]

19. He is not worth calling a theologian who seeks to interpret the invisible things of God on the basis of the things that have been created.

This is clear from those theologians . . . described as fools by the Apostle in Romans 1:22: "Professing themselves to be wise they were made fools." . . .

20. But he is worth calling a theologian who understands the visible and rearward [an allusion to Ex. 33:23] parts of God to mean [suffering] and the cross.

God determined on the contrary to be known from sufferings. He sought to condemn that sort of knowledge of the things invisible which was based on a wisdom from things visible. So that in this way those who did not worship God as made known in his works, might worship him hidden behind his sufferings. For thus he says in 1 Corinthians 1:21: "For seeing that in the wisdom of God the world did not know God by means of its wisdom, it was God's good pleasure to save those who believe by the foolishness of the preaching." From now on it could never be enough for a man, nor could it benefit him, to know God in his glory and majesty unless he knows him at the same time in the humility and shame of the cross. In this way he destroys the wisdom of the wise and brings to nought the understanding of the prudent. As Isaiah says, "Verily thou art a hidden God" (Isaiah 45:15).

Thus in John 14 when Philip asks in the spirit of the theology of glory, "Show us the Father," Christ immediately pulled him up sharp. He took him with his high-flying ideas of seeking God somewhere else and led Philip right

---

1. Luther, *Early Theological Works,* ed. James Atkinson (London: SCM, 1962), 290–92.

back to himself, saying, "Philip, whosoever sees me sees my Father as well." Therefore in Christ crucified is the true theology and the knowledge of God. He says elsewhere also, "No man comes to the Father except through me" (John 14:6). . . . .

21. The theologian of glory says bad is good and good is bad. The theologian of the cross calls them by their proper name.

This is really quite clear, for as long as a man does not know Christ he does not know God as hidden in sufferings. Such a man, therefore, prefers works to sufferings, and glory to a cross: he prefers powers to weakness, wisdom to foolishness. . . . These are they the Apostle calls enemies of the cross of Christ. Quite clearly, because they hate the cross and sufferings and certainly love works and the glory that goes with them. And thus they say that the good of the cross is evil, and call the evil of works good. But God is not to be found except in sufferings and in the cross as has been stated already. . . . It is impossible for a man not to be inflated by his own good works unless the experience of suffering and evil, having previously taken all the spirit out of him and broken him, has taught him that he is nothing and his works are not his own but God's.

22. The sort of wisdom which sees the invisible things of God in known good works simply inflates a man, and renders him both blind and hard.

This has been said already. For since it is clear that they know nothing about the cross and even hate it, then of necessity they love the opposite, that is wisdom, glory, power and the like. . . .

He who wishes to become wise should not go forward and seek wisdom but should become a fool, go back and seek foolishness. Thus, he who wants to become powerful and famous, to have a good time and enjoy all the good things of life, let him flee from power, fame, enjoyment and a sufficiency of everything and not seek after them. This is the wisdom we are talking about, the wisdom which is foolishness to the world.

The question Luther is addressing is this: How can we know God? There are some visible things humanity could look at: creation, spiritual experiences, miracles. But Luther says that they do not reveal God. Or, rather, they reveal something of God, but it is the kind of knowledge that puffs people up. As a result, people never get beyond their pride to know the real God. This knowledge could "never be enough for a man, nor could it benefit him" (20). People like this think they have knowledge, but they do not—they are fools.

Is God then unknowable? If we cannot know him through what is visible, then can we know him at all? Are we left trying to know God through what is invisible? That is not very promising, because we cannot see it! Luther's answer is this: God is known through what is *contrary*. He is known in a *hidden* way. God's invisible attributes are revealed in suffering and the cross: glory in shame, wisdom in folly, power in weakness, victory in defeat. God is known through the message of the cross.

So what Luther calls *theologia crucis*, "the theology of the cross," is not so much an understanding of how the cross saves us (though, of course, that mattered to Luther). Even more, it is an approach to knowing God. It claims that knowing him starts with the cross. And this starting point turns all our notions of God and how he can be known upside down.

The theology of the cross stems from Luther's understanding of righteousness and justification. Luther's great realization was that God justified sinners. God declares to be just those who are unjust. Luther realized that if that is so, human notions of justice can never lead us to understand God's justice. God's justice is revealed in the opposite of justice: in the justification of the unjust. Alister McGrath says:

> Luther's discovery of the "wonderful new definition of righteousness" is essentially programmatic, and capable of being applied to other divine attributes . . . leading ultimately to the *theologia crucis*, the "theology of the cross". . . .
> . . . For Luther, the "righteousness of God" is revealed exclusively in the cross, contradicting human preconceptions and expectations of the form that revelation should take.[2]

If knowledge of God could be obtained from what is visible (creation, spiritual experiences, miracles), it would lead to pride. Imagine if we knew God through creation. The people who knew him best would be those with the brains to understand the science of the universe. Or imagine we knew God through spiritual experience. The people who knew God would be those wealthy enough to spend time in contemplation. People would be able to say, "I know God through my intelligence or my spirituality or my morality or my power." It would lead to pride, and this pride would then obscure the glory and grace of God.

But God determined that he would be known through suffering so that he would be hidden from all those who exalt themselves. Here Luther is echoing the words of Jesus in Matthew 11:25–26: "I thank you, Father, Lord of heaven and earth, that you have hidden these things from the wise and

---

2. Alister McGrath, *Iustitia Dei: A History of the Christian Doctrine of Justification: From 1500 to the Present Day* (Cambridge: Cambridge University Press, 1986), 7–8.

understanding and revealed them to little children; yes, Father, for such was your gracious will."

The opposite of the theology of the cross are theologies of glory. The theologians of glory pursue wisdom, experience, and miracles and say that suffering is bad. But the theologian of the cross values suffering as that through which God is revealed. Knowledge of God is not found through human wisdom, human powers, or human achievements. It is found in the foolishness of the cross.

The religious leaders at the cross are like theologians of glory. They think God will reveal himself in a powerful act in which Jesus comes down from the cross (Mark 15:29–32). But by faith the centurion sees God revealed in the suffering and abandonment of Jesus (Mark 15:39).

Luther talks about God's "alien work," *opus alienum*, his actions which are alien to his nature, but by which he achieves his "proper work," *opus proprium*. Sometimes God assaults us in order to break us. In this light, suffering can be seen as a gracious divine gift.

Only someone who has had "all the spirit [taken] out of him and [been] broken" can know God. Often Luther is translated as saying that "humility" is the precondition for knowing God. But the word is really "humiliation." Only someone who is humiliated before God can truly know him. In other words, Luther is not commending a certain type of piety that paves the way to a better understanding of God. He is saying that we have to come to the end of ourselves before we accept God's gracious revelation. In another context Luther gave this advice to those who aspired to study theology:

> I want you to know how to study theology in the right way. I have practiced this method myself. . . . The method of which

I am speaking is the one which the holy king David teaches in Psalm 119. . . . Here you will find three rules. They are frequently proposed throughout the psalm and run thus: *oratio, meditatio, tentatio* [prayer, meditation, trials].[3]

Trials are a key way in which we learn the truth about God. Luther had in mind verses like these:

Before I was afflicted I went astray,
    but now I keep your word. (Ps. 119:67)

It is good for me that I was afflicted,
    that I might learn your statutes. (Ps. 119:71)

I know, O LORD, that your rules are righteous,
    and that in faithfulness you have afflicted me.
      (Ps. 119:75)

It is often trials that move knowledge from our heads and embed it in our hearts.

Luther was skeptical about the value of philosophy in theology. "Theology is heaven, yes even the kingdom of heaven; man however is earth and his speculations are smoke."[4] Luther, never knowingly understated, described "reason" as the Devil's whore, a beast and the enemy of God.[5] In fact Luther valued reason in matters of human society. He also valued reason as a tool to order biblical material. But we cannot discover the truth about God through human reason. Quite the opposite—reason leads us astray because the God revealed in the cross is contrary to human expectations.

---

3. Brian G. Hedges, *Christ Formed in You: The Power of the Gospel for Personal Change* (Wapwallopen, PA: Shepherd, 2010), 223.

4. *D. Martin Luthers Werke: Kritische Gesamtausgabe* (Weimar: Böhlau, 1833–), 9:65, cited in Timothy George, *Theology of the Reformers* (Nashville: Broadman; Leicester: Apollos, 1988), 57.

5. Ibid., 58.

Instead, to recognize God in the absence of God, to recognize victory in defeat, to recognize glory in shame requires *faith*. God is known only by faith. And because knowing him requires faith, this is an act of grace.

So God can be known only by those to whom he gives faith. Salvation is by grace alone. We are used to that idea. But it is the same for our knowledge of God. It is not just our salvation that is by faith alone and grace alone. We do not contribute to our knowledge of God. It is all God's doing. Our knowledge of God is by grace alone. You do not know God because you were cleverer than other people or have greater spiritual insight or spend more time in contemplation. You know God because he has graciously revealed himself to you in the message of the cross. It is an act of grace. God reveals himself in a hidden way in order to safeguard the graciousness of revelation.

So the cross subverts all human notions of glory. The message we proclaim—the message of Christ crucified—is foolishness and weakness in the sight of the world. This is Paul's point in 1 Corinthians. Indeed, in many ways Luther's theology of the cross often feels like an extended meditation of 1 Corinthians 1. In 1:23–25 we read:

> We preach Christ crucified, a stumbling block to Jews and folly to Gentiles, but to those who are called, both Jews and Greeks, Christ the power of God and the wisdom of God. For the foolishness of God is wiser than men, and the weakness of God is stronger than men.

And with this foolish, weak message of the cross goes a foolish, weak community of the cross.

> But God chose what is foolish in the world to shame the wise; God chose what is weak in the world to shame

the strong; God chose what is low and despised in the world, even things that are not, to bring to nothing things that are, so that no human being might boast in the presence of God. (1:27–29)

So the cross leaves no scope for human boasting. Instead our one boast is in Christ Jesus, "who became to us wisdom from God, righteousness and sanctification and redemption." Therefore, "Let the one who boasts, boast in the Lord" (1:30–31).

Let us summarize the key features of Luther's theology of the cross:[6]

1. The theology of the cross is a theology of *revelation*. It stands in contrast to speculation. Any notions about God we might come to through speculation on creation or experience are subverted by the revelation of God in the cross.
2. The revelation of God in the cross is a *hidden* revelation. It is indirect. It is revelation, but it is not immediately recognizable as a revelation of God.
3. The revelation of God is found in the cross of Christ. It is *not* found through *human works or reason*. Revelation through suffering shatters all our pretensions to know God through human reason or human morality.
4. God is therefore known only by *faith*. He can be discerned only by faith.
5. God is particularly known through *suffering*. It is not just that God can be known through suffering, but that he uses suffering to make himself known. And for Luther this encompasses both the sufferings of Christ and the sufferings of the individual. God humiliates us so that we may know him.

---

6. Following Alister McGrath, *Luther's Theology of the Cross* (Oxford: Blackwell, 1985), 148–52, who in turn follows W. von Loewenich, *Luthers Theologia Crucis* (Munich: Luther-Verlag, 1954).

Why the Theology of the Cross Still Matters

Given this foundation, much Protestant theology took a surprising turn in the eighteenth and nineteenth centuries. It turned toward what became known as "liberal theology." Catholicism, too, was not immune to this movement. In effect, large parts of Protestant mainline denominations and Western Catholicism opted for a theology of glory.

Liberalism was the theological counterpart of the Enlightenment, the intellectual movement that has shaped the modern world. Its chief characteristic was its emphasis on human reason. Human reason was seen as the solution to human ignorance (epistemology) and the solution to human problems (soteriology). When it came to divine revelation, reason was no longer a tool to assist our understanding of the Bible. Reason was now the ultimate source of truth. In his book *Christianity as Old as Creation* (1730) Matthew Tindal sought to establish knowledge of God on the basis of rational observance of the world. The result was not the God of the Bible but the god of deism—a god who is uninvolved in the world he has made. No longer would revelation judge human reason. Human reason would now judge revelation. And so the so-called higher biblical criticism was born, which gradually removed from the Bible any unity, historicity, reliability, and authority.

The hope was that through shared human reason humanity could agree on what is true. Through a process of rational enquiry we could find a shared basis for human society. Postmodernism rightly rebels against this false hope. Human reason is corrupted by sin. In postmodern terms, truth is a function of power. Claims to absolute truth are often used by the powerful to maintain their position of power.

But postmodernism is still very much part of the Enlightenment. It is perhaps the latest manifestation of romanticism. Romanticism reacted against the cold logic of reason with an emphasis on spiritual and aesthetic experiences. Knowledge was found from within. The emphasis was not so much on human reason as on human experience. But knowledge was still a human endeavor. We have the capacity to determine truth for ourselves. So romanticism and postmodernism are more a stream within the Enlightenment than a reaction to it.

What reason and romanticism, modernity and postmodernity have in common is the autonomous self. The rationalism of the Enlightenment is about autonomous human reason. Romanticism is about autonomous human experience. Postmodernity is about autonomous individuals determining truth for themselves. Tradition is not about autonomous individuals but about an autonomous community of human beings. What they all have in common is a human-centered approach to knowledge. Knowledge is grounded in human beings—our tradition or our reason or our experience or, in the case of postmodernity, our will (maybe even our whim).

But for Luther the theology of the cross judges all such presumptuous claims. The cross exposes our sin. In Catholic thought, nature and grace are on a continuum in which grace may complete nature. In other words, our natural knowledge is supplemented by grace. In modern thought grace is not required. Natural reason alone is sufficient. But the theology of the cross takes sin seriously. Sin has corrupted our reason. We are still rational beings. We are still capable of discovery and invention. But our reason is captive to our sinful desires. We instinctively bend our reason to justify our actions (Rom. 1:18–25).

But when we stand before the cross, we are humbled. Our sinful biases are exposed. The gift of faith opens our eyes to see glory in shame, power in weakness, victory in defeat. We learn to trust divine revelation more than human reason.

A confidence in God's revelation in Scripture is one of the defining features of evangelicalism. It is no accident that the other defining feature is penal substitution, the conviction that on the cross Jesus, in our place, bore the penalty of divine wrath that we deserve. Both features recognize the limits of human ability and magnify the glory of divine grace. The cross is central to our understanding of revelation and salvation.

The Disciples of the Cross

But the challenge of the theology of the cross comes closer to home. For the cross defines not only how we think but also how we live.

Luther developed "the theology of the cross" as the foundational principle of theological method. It was his answer to the question of how we can know God. We know him not primarily through mystical insight or theological wisdom or supernatural visions or words of knowledge or the beauty of creation. We know God through the message of the cross.

But the same answer can be applied to the question of how we know the *power* of God. We know the power of God through the message of the cross—not primarily through healing miracles or political influence or spiritual disciplines or media presence or managerial skill or megachurches or inspirational leaders or sociological theories. We need to ditch our worldly notions of success. We need to ditch our preoccupation with numbers and size. The theology of the cross still matters, and not just for theology. The whole of the Christian life here on earth is to be cruciform or cross-shaped.

The goal of the Great Commission is to "make disciples of

all nations, baptizing them in the name of the Father and of the Son and of the Holy Spirit, teaching them to observe all that I have commanded you" (Matt. 28:19–20). But in Matthew's Gospel Jesus has already defined what it means to be a disciple. "If anyone would come after me, let him deny himself and take up his cross and follow me" (Matt. 16:24). This statement comes in response to Peter's rebuke. Jesus has declared his coming death and Peter takes him aside: "Far be it from you, Lord!" he says. "This shall never happen to you" (Matt. 16:22). Peter wants the glory of the kingdom without the cross. Jesus responds, literally, "Go behind me, Satan," echoing his words "Go, Satan" in the wilderness when Satan offered him the kingdom without the cross (Matt. 4:8–10).

The pattern of New Testament discipleship is the pattern of suffering followed by glory, reflecting the pattern of the cross and resurrection. Peter learned his lesson well. He says that the Spirit predicted in the Old Testament "the sufferings of Christ and the subsequent glories" (1 Pet. 1:11). In 1 Peter 2–3 Peter outlines what it means for Christians to live good lives in a pagan world—lives with missiological implications, for they lead to people glorifying God (2:11–12). He explores Christian responsibility toward the state (2:13–17), in the workplace (2:18–20), and within marriage (3:1–7). Peter talks about how we should respond when we suffer for doing good (3:8–22). Central to all of this teaching is the example laid down by the cross (2:21–25). Christian discipleship is to be shaped by the cross and its model of sacrificial love. The cross exemplifies the calling that slaves have received (2:21), while wives and husbands are told to act "likewise" (3:1, 7), that is, in the way of the cross. The cross is our pattern. Jesus did not retaliate against evil but responded with good (2:23; 3:9). He died, the righteous for the unrighteous—and we are the unrighteous for whom he died. He responded to our rejection with an act that brings us to God (3:18). Now we respond to rejection with an eagerness to do good (3:13–17).

But the pattern of the cross is only half the picture. We follow the way of the cross in the hope of resurrection glory. Peter tells us to "rejoice insofar as you share Christ's sufferings, that you may also rejoice and be glad when his glory is revealed" (1 Pet. 4:13). At the end of the letter Peter says that he has written to testify to "the true grace of God" (5:12). What is the true grace of God? It is the grace that Peter has defined in the previous verses: "And after you have suffered a little while, the God of all grace, who has called you to his eternal glory in Christ, will himself restore, confirm, strengthen, and establish you. To him be the dominion forever and ever. Amen" (5:10–11). This true grace is the ability to suffer for a little while in the hope of eternal glory and restoration.

What completes the picture is the Holy Spirit. Through the Spirit we have resurrection life and power now. But resurrection power is given to us that we may live the life of the cross. It is power to be weak (2 Cor. 4:7–12; Phil. 3:10–11). Our resurrection life is a hidden life, revealed in conformity with Christ and his cross (Col. 3:1–4). The Christian life is not a life of victory and power, but nor is it simply a life of weakness. It is a life of *power in weakness*, a life lived in conscious dependence upon the power of God mediated by the Holy Spirit.

So, just as there are dangerous theologies of glory, there are also dangerous eschatologies of glory. Eschatology is the doctrine of Christian hope and the last times. The last times began with the first coming of Jesus and will be brought to their completion at his return. So eschatology is not just about what happens in the future. It is also about how we understand life now.

Eschatologies of glory seek the glory and victory of the

resurrection without accepting the reality of the cross in the present. This was the mistake made by James and John. They wanted glory without suffering, so they came to Jesus asking for positions of honor in his kingdom. But Jesus responded by telling them they first had to suffer with him (Mark 10:35–45).

Instead of eschatologies of glory we must embrace an eschatology of the cross that looks forward to glory and victory while seeing them as present now in a hidden form of shame and weakness. The cross judges overrealized eschatologies of individual victory and success such as those proposed by the prosperity gospel. "Through many tribulations we must enter the kingdom of God" (Acts 14:22). But the cross also judges the overrealized eschatologies of social utopians and revolutionaries. Hope must be accompanied by patient endurance.

Paul says, "I consider that the sufferings of this present time are not worth comparing with the glory that is to be revealed to us" (Rom. 8:18). This verse comes in the middle of Romans 8—a chapter about how we square the promises of the gospel with the realities of sin, suffering, and death. The answer is in part that we are not yet what we shall be. Like the rest of creation, we await our redemption. We have hope, but "hope that is seen is not hope. For who hopes for what he sees? But if we hope for what we do not see, we wait for it with patience" (Rom. 8:24–25). Again and again in the New Testament the corollaries of hope are patience and long-suffering.

But patience and long-suffering are not common characteristics among Western Christians. Modern Westerners expect good health as a norm. We call for public inquiries because we think every disaster can be avoided. And we Christians are not so very different. We expect God to keep us healthy and safe. So when trouble comes, as Jesus promised it will (John 16:33), we not only struggle to cope with the problem; we cannot make sense of what God is doing. Why does he not answer my prayers? Is my faith too weak? The result is that people struggling with turmoil in the circumstances of their lives are beset at the same time with a crisis of faith. No wonder, then, that Paul prays Christians will realize "the hope to which he has called you" (Eph. 1:18).

This pattern of suffering followed by glory also features strongly in the theology of John Calvin, and especially his understanding of our union with Christ. Union with Christ is one of his controlling themes, and that means union with Christ in his death and resurrection. "The resurrection does not lead us away from the cross."[7] Our redemption remains hidden until the day Christ returns, the day of "revelation." Although adopted by God, justified, forgiven, and renewed by the Holy Spirit, Christians do not yet *appear* any more blessed than others, except to the extent that their hidden hope expresses itself in joy and confidence in God. Indeed, Christians more often appear worse off because of their commitment to the way of the cross.

Our participation in the resurrection and life of Christ and our inward life in the Spirit are not outwardly discernible. Or, rather, they manifest themselves outwardly in our commitment to the way of the cross.

The Swiss theologian Emil Brunner says:

> The whole history of Christianity, and the history of the world as a whole, would have followed a different course if it had not been that again and again a *theologia crucis* [a theology of the cross] became the *theologia gloriae* [a theology of glory], and that the *ecclesia crucis* [a church of the cross] became an *ecclesia gloriae* [a church of glory].[8]

---

7. Calvin, *Commentary*, on Gal. 6:14.
8. Emil Brunner, *The Mediator* (London: Lutterworth, 1934), 435.

The temptation is to think that what we need most are national evangelistic campaigns or megachurches with slick multimedia presentations or access to the global media or charismatic personalities or influence in the halls of power. This is not a new temptation. The church has always faced the temptation to seek power and influence in the world.

But the theology of the cross calls us to place our confidence in what Jesus calls his "little flock" (Luke 12:32). At the heart of Jesus's future are not globalized ecclesial structures—whether the Catholic magisterium or pan-evangelical networks. Instead the future belongs to small unassuming churches—Christ's little flock. It is to Christ's little flock that the kingdom of God has been given—the all-powerful, life-giving rule of God.

So we need not only a theology of the cross but also a church of the cross. The understanding of the church consistent with the gospel of Christ crucified is *a church of the cross*. That means power in weakness, wisdom in folly, and glory in shame. It means we must put our confidence in God rather than in ourselves. Christ is building his church, for the most part unseen, in the shape of thousands of small congregations. In this there is hope: the sovereignty of the risen Christ, and his "little flock."

6

Union with Christ

Who Am I?

The grand story of the Bible is a romance. It is a tale about marriage. In the beginning Adam becomes "one flesh" with Eve; at
the end we hear of the marriage supper of the Lamb and the
New Jerusalem prepared as a bride adorned for her husband.
More specifically, it is a tale about *the* marriage, about Christ
the Bridegroom and how he unites himself with his bride, the
church.

Given the importance of the theme, it should be no surprise that Christians of every generation and tradition have
thought and taught about this union with Christ. Roman
Catholic and Protestant theologians, pre-Reformation and
Reformation theologians—all have accepted union with
Christ as part of the gospel. However, there was and is a
world of difference between them as to what exactly union
with Christ *means*.

Union with Christ in Medieval Roman Catholicism

The medieval theologian most associated with union with Christ was Bernard of Clairvaux (1090–1153), and partly for that very reason he was highly esteemed by both Luther and Calvin. His most famous work was a series of eighty-six sermons, *Sermons on the Song of Songs*—a series he failed to complete before dying. At the time Song of Solomon was a highly popular text of choice for preachers and was universally read as a parable of Christ's love for his church. Here in his third sermon, imagining a mystical encounter between the believer and Jesus, is how Bernard would describe union with Christ:

> *Growth in grace brings expansion of confidence.* You will love with greater ardour, and knock on the door with greater assurance, in order to gain what you perceive to be still wanting to you. "The one who knocks will always have the door opened to him." It is my belief that *to a person so disposed*, God will not refuse that most intimate kiss of all, a mystery of supreme generosity and ineffable sweetness. You have seen the way that we must follow, the order of procedure: first, we cast ourselves at his feet, we weep before the Lord who made us, deploring the evil we have done. Then we reach out for the hand that will lift us up, that will steady our trembling knees. And finally, *when we shall have obtained these favours through many prayers and tears*, we humbly dare to raise our eyes to his mouth, so divinely beautiful, not merely to gaze upon it, but—I say it with fear and trembling—to receive its kiss. "Christ the Lord is a Spirit before our face," and he who is joined to him in a holy kiss becomes through his good pleasure, one spirit with him.[1]

---

1. Bernard of Clairvaux, sermon 3.5, in *On the Song of Songs* (Kalamazoo, MI: Cistercian, 1979), 154–55 (emphases added).

The unashamed physicality of the language, of one person seeking a "most intimate kiss" with another, stops many today from seeing the point. Yet that burning desire for Christ is just what the Reformers appreciated about Bernard. He *longed* for union with Christ. Still, though, Bernard was working with a medieval Roman Catholic understanding of that union. For him union was a *fluid* state: you could be *more* or *less* united to Christ. Hence he could imagine an "order of procedure" whereby through "many prayers and tears" (and sacraments) the Christian could get ever closer to Christ until perfect union.

Union with Christ in the Reformation

That was not at all how the mainstream Reformers thought of union with Christ. For them there was an important difference between *union* and *communion*. Communion with Christ— meaning the actual enjoyment of Christ—is something that fluctuates in believers. Sometimes our hearts are full of hallelujahs; sometimes they are frosty and unfeeling toward him. That wavering warmth of communion, however, was not seen by the Reformers as the foundation or essence of our union with Christ. Quite the opposite. The Puritan Richard Sibbes, in perhaps the most notable work on the Song of Solomon written from the point of view of the Reformation, put it like this: "*Union is the foundation of communion.*"[2] In Reformation thought, union with Christ is a fixed and therefore stable thing, the solid foundation on which we can know lasting joy.

The difference between *union* and *communion* for the Reformers stemmed from their strong belief in the centrality of Christ, the source and substance of all good. According to John Calvin,

---

2. Richard Sibbes, "Bowels Opened," in *The Complete Works of Richard Sibbes*, ed. Alexander B. Grosart, 7 vols. (Edinburgh: James Nichol, 1862–1864), 2:174 (emphasis added).

it is indisputable that no one is loved by God apart from Christ: "This is the beloved Son," in whom dwells and rests the Father's love. And from him it then pours itself upon us, just as Paul teaches: "We receive grace in the beloved" [Eph. 1:6].[3]

That first sentence could make God sound nastily exclusive—and it would not have been good news at all for us if Calvin had stopped there. His point is that God does not have some quantity of love that has to be divided up and shared out among all the world's believers, living and dead. If that were the case, I would reason that God *cannot* love me that much—and I might as well try to win his attention with a few works. Instead God gives *all* the fullness of his love to his Son, and from him *all* that fullness pours down upon us. God loves us with the unbounded love he has for his Son.

So where Bernard imagined the Christian striving forward in the passionate *hope* of attaining full union with Christ, Calvin saw the Christian life *starting* with union with Christ. For Calvin a key image would be that of the vine: Jesus Christ is the Vine, filled with the love and life of God. Unattached to him we have no spiritual life whatsoever. But "engrafted" into him like branches, we have, undissipated, all the life and love he enjoys.

How do we receive those benefits which the Father bestowed on his only-begotten Son—not for Christ's own private use, but that he might enrich poor and needy men? First, we must understand that as long as Christ remains outside of us, and we are separated from him, all that he has suffered and done for the salvation of the human race remains useless and of no value for us. Therefore, to share with us what he has received from the Father, he had to

---

3. Calvin, *Institutes*, 3.2.32.

become ours and to dwell within us. For this reason, he is called "our Head" [Eph. 4:15], and "the first-born among many brethren" [Rom. 8:29]. We also, in turn, are said to be "engrafted into him" [Rom. 11:17], and to "put on Christ" [Gal. 3:27]; for, as I have said, all that he possesses is nothing to us until we grow into one body with him.[4]

But

as soon as you become engrafted into Christ through faith, you are made a son of God, an heir of heaven, a partaker in righteousness, a possessor of life; and . . . you obtain not the opportunity to gain merit but all the merits of Christ, for they are communicated to you.[5]

As far as Calvin saw it, then, there can be no gospel without union with Christ. The Son of God—God himself—became "God with us" precisely so that he might be one with us. He then gives us his Spirit that we may be one with him. "For this is the design of the gospel, that Christ may become ours, and that we may be ingrafted into his body."[6]

Righteous in Christ

For Calvin and the mainstream Reformers union with Christ was the radical solution we need, given the radical problem of sin. In Romans 5 Paul writes that

sin came into the world through one man, and death through sin. . . .

---

4. Calvin, *Institutes*, 3.1.1.
5. Calvin, *Institutes*, 3.15.6.
6. Calvin, *Commentary*, on 1 Cor. 1:9. "The end of the whole Gospel ministry is that God, the fountain of all felicity, communicate Christ to us who are disunited by sin and hence ruined, that we may from him enjoy eternal life; that in a word all heavenly treasures be so applied to us that they be no less ours than Christ's himself" (J. K. S. Reid, ed., *Calvin: Theological Treatises*, Library of Christian Classics 22 [Philadelphia: Westminster, 1954], 171).

> . . . because of one man's trespass, death reigned through
> that one man. . . .
>   . . . one trespass led to condemnation for all men. . . .
> by the one man's disobedience the many were made sinners.
> (5:12, 17–19)

In other words, the problem of our sin goes deeper than our
individual acts of sin and further back even than our birth. We
were born of Adam, and so were born sharing his (doomed)
status and his (sinful) inclinations. This means it is not enough
for us to have the record of our sinful acts expunged, or for
us to be given a boost to do better: we must be *born again*. As
we were born of Adam, united to him and sharing his status
and inclinations, so we must be born again of Christ, sharing
his status and inclinations. "For as *in Adam* all die, so also *in
Christ* shall all be made alive" (1 Cor. 15:22).

Far better than having a few sins washed away, those who
are reborn in Christ and so united to him can cry out with Paul,
"I have been crucified with Christ. It is no longer I who live, but
Christ who lives in me" (Gal. 2:20). For if we are united to him,
then we have been united to him in his death: "In the cross of
our Lord Jesus Christ . . . the world has been crucified to me,
and I to the world" (Gal. 6:14; see Rom. 6:3; Col. 2:12). In him
we have died to sin, we have been crucified and condemned, we
have already endured the full punishment for it all. Moreover,
we share the vindication he received on the third day when he
was raised again, declared righteous, and accepted (Rom. 4:25;
1 Tim. 3:16). United to him, we share his new life and the very
righteousness of God (2 Cor. 5:21; see 1 Cor. 1:30).

The idea that believers are credited with the righteousness
of Christ was quickly pooh-poohed by Roman Catholic theologians as a dubious and therefore flimsy legal fiction. And

certainly it can *seem* rather questionable. As a young Christian, I remember puzzling over how my sin could be transferred to the cross, and Jesus's righteousness conferred to me. I liked the idea, but since sin and righteousness are not commodities we can package up and pass around, how, I wondered, could such a swap be any more than a pipe dream? Tom Wright drolly shows how chucklesome the idea can be:

> If we use the language of the law court, it makes no sense whatever to say that the judge imputes, imparts, bequeaths, conveys or otherwise transfers his righteousness to either the plaintiff or the defendant. Righteousness is not an object, a substance or a gas which can be passed across the courtroom.[7]

But if Christ takes our sin and we take his righteousness *because we are united to him*, then all those difficulties melt away. As Calvin would argue, "We do not, therefore, contemplate him [Christ] outside ourselves from afar in order that his righteousness may be imputed to us but because we put on Christ and are engrafted into his body—in short, because he deigns to make us one with him."[8] If Christ and the believer are made *one*, then the sin righteousness swap is as unobjectionable as what happens in a marriage when a man and woman become *one*. In a marriage the husband shares all he has with his wife and she shares all she has with him. It is as if a rich husband were—at his own cost—to pay off all his wife's debts and then share with her his enormous wealth. It was, in fact, just this image that Martin Luther used to explain how we receive the righteousness of Christ:

---

7. N. T. Wright, *What St Paul Really Said* (Oxford: Lion, 1997), 98.
8. Calvin, *Institutes*, 3.11.10. Elsewhere he would explain, "You see that our righteousness is not in us but in Christ, that we possess it only because we are partakers in Christ" (*Institutes*, 3.11.23).

But faith must be taught correctly, namely, that by it you are so cemented to Christ that He and you are as one person, which cannot be separated but remains attached to Him forever and declares: "I am as Christ." And Christ, in turn, says: "I am as that sinner who is attached to Me, and I to him. For by faith we are joined together into one flesh and one bone." Thus Eph. 5:30 says: "We are members of the body of Christ, of His flesh and of His bones," in such a way that this faith couples Christ and me more intimately than a husband is coupled to his wife.[9]

This was a true Copernican revolution in theology, and all who come to believe this *feel* how it throws everything happily head over heels. We naturally have ourselves at the center of our own solar system. Christianity, we assume, must be all about how *I* am doing. Being a Christian is like having Christ in *my* orbit. Which seems fine—when I am doing well. The rest of the time I must worry: Have I prayed enough? Have I sinned too much? Can God still love me after *that*? The Reformation instead placed *Christ* at the center, replacing fitful anxiety with stable joy. For instead of asking, "How righteous am I?" to know how I stand before God, I ask, "How righteous is Christ?" And then I smile. For amid my ups and downs he is utterly righteous, yesterday, today, and forever—and all his is mine.

Of course, this is news so rip-roaringly good we rub our eyes in amazement, imagine we have been dreaming, and then return to our old way of thinking. And so, ever since the days of the Reformation, it has been a staple of Protestant ministry to urge people to *remember* and hold fast to this sweet message day by day. Preaching to his congregation in Victorian London, Charles Spurgeon implored:

---

9. *Luther's Works*, 26:168.

Remember that *he sees us now in Christ*. Behold, he has put his people into the hands of his dear Son. He has even put us into Christ's body; "for we are members of his body, of his flesh, and of his bones." He sees us in Christ to have died, in him to have been buried, and in him to have risen again. As the Lord Jesus Christ is well-pleasing to the Father, so in him are we well-pleasing to the Father also; for our being in him identifies us with him. If, then, our acceptance with God stands on the footing of Christ's acceptance with God, it standeth firmly, and is an unchanging argument with the Lord God for doing us good. If we stood before God in our own individual righteousness, our ruin would be sure and speedy; but in Jesus our life is hid beyond peril. Firmly believe that until the Lord rejects Christ he cannot reject his people; until he repudiates the atonement and the resurrection, he cannot cast away any of those with whom he has entered into covenant in the Lord Jesus Christ.[10]

Adopted in Christ

Union with Christ was never treated by the Reformers as the mere engine under the hood of justification and no more. Rather, they believed, *all* the blessings of the gospel are ours because of our union with Christ. Christ shares all he has with us through making us one with himself. Summing up Christ's redeeming work, Calvin writes:

His task was so to restore us to God's grace as to make of the children of men, children of God; of the heirs of Gehenna, heirs of the Heavenly Kingdom. Who could have done this had not the self-same Son of God become the Son of man, and had not so taken what was ours as to impart

---

10. C. H. Spurgeon, *The Metropolitan Tabernacle Pulpit Sermons*, vol. 35 (London: Passmore & Alabaster, 1889), 547 (emphasis original).

what was his to us, and to make what was his by nature ours by grace?[11]

In other words, the Son of God does not merely share with us what could sound like some cold access card, "Righteousness." He shares with us his own sonship. Through making us one with him, he "has adopted us as his brothers"[12] so that we can share his Spirit-filled cry of "Abba" (Rom. 8:14–17; Gal. 4:6–7). Because of our union with Christ we have the Son's own Comforter, the Spirit, who helps us; because of our union with Christ, we can daily call out to an omnipotent Father, knowing that he yearns to hear us, accepting us entirely in his well-beloved Son.

Transformed in Christ

You can probably guess what critics of the Reformation said about all this. That this is a doctrine of comfort was precisely the problem, they said, for this message is simply *too* comforting. If our anxieties about our guilt and standing before God can be washed away so freely in Christ, what possible motivation are we left with to pursue lives of holiness? But, understanding that salvation *is* union with Christ, Calvin was not troubled for a moment, and replied as follows:

> If he who has obtained justification possesses Christ, and at the same time, Christ never is where His Spirit is not, it is obvious that gratuitous righteousness is necessarily connected with regeneration. Therefore, if you would duly understand how inseparable faith and works are, look to Christ, who, as the Apostle teaches (1 Cor. i. 30) has been given to us for justification and for sanctification. Wherever,

---

11. Calvin, *Institutes*, 2.12.2.
12. Calvin, *Institutes*, 2.12.2.

therefore, that righteousness of faith, which we maintain to be gratuitous, is, there too Christ is, and where Christ is, there too is the Spirit of holiness, who regenerates the soul to newness of life. On the contrary, where zeal for integrity and holiness is not in vigor, there neither is the Spirit of Christ nor Christ Himself; and wherever Christ is not, there is no righteousness, nay, there is no faith; for faith cannot apprehend Christ for righteousness without the Spirit of sanctification.[13]

That is, we have not been united to Christ so we can get some *other* reward: heaven, righteousness, salvation, or whatever. We do not, as Calvin put it, seek "in Christ something else than Christ himself."[14] The great reward of union with Christ is *Christ*. Knowing and enjoying him *is* the eternal life for which we have been saved. It is why, in his earliest days as a young believer, Calvin began identifying himself as "a lover of Jesus Christ."

The total gratuity of our salvation does not mean that the doctrine of union with Christ ignores how we then live. The apostle Paul writes that "we were buried therefore with him by baptism into death, *in order that*, just as Christ was raised from the dead by the glory of the Father, we too might walk in newness of life" (Rom. 6:4). In Christ we receive his righteousness and sonship, *and* in Christ we receive his transforming life and Spirit. Martin Luther wrote that "through faith in Christ, Christ's righteousness becomes our righteousness and all that he has becomes ours; *rather, He Himself becomes ours*."[15] United to him, sharing his life, and filled with his Spirit, we cannot but be transformed to be more like him. The new life and new

---

13. John Calvin and Jacopo Sadoleto, *A Reformation Debate*, ed. John C. Olin (1966; repr., Fordham University Press, 2000), 62.

14. Calvin, *Commentary*, on John 6:26.

15. *Luther's Works*, 31:298 (emphasis added).

heart we have been given in Christ begin to show. "And we all, with unveiled face, beholding the glory of the Lord, are being transformed into the same image from one degree of glory to another. For this comes from the Lord who is the Spirit" (2 Cor. 3:18).

The biblical image that makes this clearest is that of Christ the Vine, with believers as his branches (John 15:1–8). There believers are depicted as one with Christ, who pours the life-giving sap of the Spirit into us, making us fruitful. In that image Jesus could not have made it clearer that our union with him is deeply transformative. Luther commented on this:

> To summarize, the very essence of my heart is renewed and changed. This makes me a new plant, one that is grafted on Christ the Vine and grows from Him. My holiness, righteousness, and purity do not stem from me, nor do they depend on me. They come solely from Christ and are based only in Him, in whom I am rooted by faith, just as the sap flows from the stalk into the branches. Now I am like Him and of His kind. Both He and I are of one nature and essence, and I bear fruit in Him and through Him. This fruit is not mine; it is the Vine's.[16]

The fact that Christians are united to Christ and share his life *must* affect them. We have not been given a "saved" status and then left to get on with holy lives all by ourselves. If we are united to Christ, we have a new heart and a new Spirit within us.

But it is good for us to ponder our union with Christ regularly and often. For all too easily I forget that Christ has become my identity, and I think I *am* what I *do*. And that is just when things start to go wrong: when I am doing well, I then

---

16. *Luther's Works*, 24:226.

become proud and unbearable; when I am not, I curl up in defeated misery. Either way, when I forget my union with Christ and allow other things to define me, I become ridiculous and dangerous. But when I remember that Christ defines me, I find myself much more immune to both pride and failure. In him I am no failure at all, but triumphant. In him what have I to be proud of but him?

Christ in You, the Hope of Glory

The reason we are able to forget our union with Christ is that we have yet to experience the full glory of what it *will* mean. For now, we are members of Christ's body, but we still wander, our bodies still ache, and we shall still die. "But our citizenship is in heaven, and from it we await a Savior, the Lord Jesus Christ, who will transform our lowly body to be like his glorious body, by the power that enables him even to subject all things to himself" (Phil. 3:20–21). Christ is our Bridegroom who will not desert us; he is our Head who has blazed a trail to glory that his body must follow. That being the case, John Calvin was prepared to use striking language to explain the love of Christ for his people:

> This is the highest honour of the Church, that, until he is united to us, the Son of God reckons himself in some measure imperfect. What consolation is it for us to learn, that, not until we are along with him, does he possess all his parts, or wish to be regarded as complete![17]

Our Only Comfort

Naturally the theologians and leaders of the Reformation were keen as mustard to ensure that as many as possible understood

---

17. Calvin, *Commentary*, on Eph. 1:23.

this wonderful news. Before long, then, a good number of them were writing question-and-answer catechisms to help people digest this Reformational theology. Perhaps the best-known of all was the Heidelberg Catechism (1563), which puts union with Christ front and center in its first question, unfurling what comfort we can know from being *in Christ*:

> What is your only comfort in life and death? That I, with body and soul, both in life and in death, am not my own, but belong to my faithful Saviour Jesus Christ, who with his precious blood has fully satisfied for all my sins, and redeemed me from all the power of the devil; and so preserves me that without the will of my Father in heaven not a hair can fall from my head; yea, that all things must work together for my salvation. Wherefore, by his Holy Spirit, he also assures me of eternal life, and makes me heartily willing and ready henceforth to live unto him.[18]

Small wonder the Reformers believed they had rediscovered truth for every generation, truth that brings life, truth worth dying for!

---

18. "The Heidelberg Catechism," in *The School of Faith: The Catechisms of the Reformed Church*, ed. Thomas F. Torrance (London: James Clarke, 1959), 68.

7

The Spirit

Can We Truly Know God?

Where did the Spirit go in late medieval Roman Catholicism? That is no easy question to answer, since for most of the Roman Church the sacramental system and the clergy seemed effectively to replace the Spirit. God's grace was a blessing accessed through the seven taps of the seven sacraments: baptism, confirmation, the Eucharist, penance, the anointing of the sick (including the last rites), holy orders, and matrimony. And the clergy were the ones who turned those taps on or off. With such a hermetically sealed plumbing system for grace, the Spirit was left with nothing to do.

And yet the very mechanistic tightness of it all provoked something of a resistance movement. Many wanted more: they wanted a deeper, more personal encounter with God, not just a priestly claim that grace had been given in some unintelligible church service. And so they began to look elsewhere for spiritual transformation through mystical experiences.[1] One of the many who felt indebted to this mystical subculture or counterculture was Martin Luther. In fact his first publication was an edition of an anonymously authored mystical text he would later title *A German Theology*. Apart from the Bible and Augustine, he insisted, no book had taught him more about God, Christ, and humanity. In other words, a good part of Luther's dissatisfaction with the church of his day had to do with the Spirit.

You Must Be Born Again

In many ways the Reformation as a whole would be a fight for the following line in the Nicene Creed: "We believe in the Spirit, the Lord, *the giver of life*." Wrapped up in that affirmation is the belief that we do not have life in ourselves. We therefore need more than a bit of enabling grace: we need *life*. As the Spirit hovered over the waters in the beginning, giving life to creation, so again we need the Spirit in order to have new life. Luther therefore wrote that the first thing belief in the Spirit means is that "by my own reason or strength I cannot believe in Jesus Christ, my Lord, or come to him. But the Holy Spirit has called me through the Gospel."[2] Salvation, in other words, cannot be a cooperative effort, God's assisting merely weak sinners; it is a divine rescue, God's raising the dead. Belief in the Spirit as the "giver of life" means belief in salvation by grace alone. For, wrote Luther, "we never read that the Holy Spirit was given to anybody because he had performed some works, but always when men have heard the gospel of Christ and the mercy of God."[3]

1. For helpful further reading on this, see Steven Ozment, *The Age of Reform, 1250–1550: An Intellectual and Religious History of Late Medieval and Reformation Europe* (New Haven, CT: Yale University Press, 1980), chaps. 2–3.

2. The Small Catechism, in *The Book of Concord: The Confessions of the Evangelical Lutheran Church*, trans. and ed. T. G. Tappert (Philadelphia: Fortress, 1959), 345.

3. *Luther's Works*, 44:30, 38–39.

The reason we do not have life is that a fault in us goes deeper than our actions. We do not have life because we do not turn to receive it from the author and source of life.

Be appalled, O heavens, at this;
    be shocked, be utterly desolate,
declares the LORD,
for my people have committed two evils:
they have forsaken me,
    the fountain of living waters,
and hewed out cisterns for themselves,
    broken cisterns that can hold no water (Jer 2:12–13)

We all long for life but naturally seek it anywhere but in him, in other relationships and other pleasures. Our hearts lean elsewhere, and so, never choosing him, we can never have life. Without the Spirit, then, we would be capable of altering ourselves superficially, but no more than that. If we are to have life, the Spirit must give us new birth into a new life by giving us new hearts that desire him and so turn to receive from him (Ezek. 36:26; John 3:3–8).

Contending for all this was right at the heart of the Reformation and meant that the Reformers believed in the need for radical, from-the-inside-out change. They saw that we stony-hearted sinners need more than mere behavioral modification. We need a deep internal reformation through the Spirit's opening our eyes to see who the Lord truly and beautifully is. We need our hearts to be overturned and melted, our love of self eclipsed by a superior enjoyment of a superlatively lovely God. That is, the Reformers believed in being born again, in God-haters being won by the gospel, not just to an outward act of obedience to God, but to love, desire, and delight in him.

The English Bible translator William Tyndale was one of

the earliest Reformers to make clear how different this belief in the living Spirit is from the superficial ritualism of his youth. He explained it like this: our problem is "the heart, with all the powers, affections, and appetites, wherewith we can but sin." Our only solution is "the Spirit, which looseth the heart."[4] Only the Spirit has the ability so to "loose" our hearts from their enslaving love of self and win them to the freedom of knowing God. Unless the believer "had felt the infinite mercy, goodness, love, and kindness of God, and the fellowship of the blood of Christ, and the comfort of the Spirit of Christ in his heart, he could never have forsaken any thing for God's sake."[5] And so, in a tract smuggled into England alongside many copies of his New Testament translation, Tyndale would advise his fellow Englishmen still trapped in ritualism:

> If thou wilt therefore be at peace with God, and love him, thou must turn to the promises of God, and to the gospel, which is called of Paul, in the place before rehearsed to the Corinthians, the ministration of righteousness, and of the Spirit. For faith bringeth pardon, and forgiveness freely purchased by Christ's blood, and bringeth also the Spirit; the Spirit looseth the bonds of the devil, and setteth us at liberty.[6]

This theology made for the most practical difference in Reformation circles. The Reformers saw that the root of our problem before God does not lie in our behavior: it is not as if we have done wrong things and simply need to start doing right things. All our outward acts of sin are merely the mani-

---

4. William Tyndale, "A Prologue upon the Epistle of St Paul to the Romans," in *The Works of William Tyndale*, 2 vols. (Cambridge: Parker Society, 1848; repr., Edinburgh: Banner of Truth, 2010), 1:489; see also Tyndale, "The Parable of the Wicked Mammon," 1:52.

5. Tyndale, "Prologue upon the Epistle to the Romans," 1:109.

6. Tyndale, "Parable of the Wicked Mammon," 1:48.

festations of the inner desires of our hearts. Therefore, merely to alter a person's behavior without dealing with those desires would only cultivate hypocrisy, the self-righteous cloak for a cold and vicious heart. And, some noted, ministers who sought only superficial, behavioral change in their people were invariably cruel browbeaters. This Reformation insight meant that hearts had to be turned, and evil desires eclipsed by stronger ones for Christ.

For such fundamental change to happen, the Reformers saw that the gospel had to be preached. Tyndale again:

> When Christ is thuswise preached . . . [hearts] begin to wax soft and melt at the bounteous mercy of God, and kindness shewed of Christ. For when the evangelion is preached, the Spirit of God entereth into them . . . and openeth their inward eyes, and worketh such belief in them. When the woful consciences feel and taste how sweet a thing the bitter death of Christ is, and how merciful and loving God is, through Christ's purchasing and merits; they begin to love.[7]

That is to say, our sin cannot be removed from our hearts simply by our trying harder or scrubbing ourselves clean: the Spirit must transform us through the gospel. That is how the new life of the Spirit begins, and that is how it grows. As Tyndale so enchantingly put it, "Where the Spirit is, there it is always summer, and there are always good fruits, that is to say, good works."[8] Left to our natural selfish coldness we can only spew forth self-glorifying, sham acts of goodness, but the heart that stays continually enlightened and refreshed by the Spirit will be warm, summery, and truly fruitful. The gospel, then, cannot be treated *simply* as a message for unbelievers, as the doorway into

---

7. William Tyndale, "A Pathway into the Holy Scripture," in *Works of William Tyndale*, 1:19.
8. Tyndale, "Prologue upon the Epistle to the Romans," 1:499.

the Christian life; in order for Christians to grow they must be *kept* in the sunshine of the gospel.

Knowing God

All this being more familiar today, it is easy to miss how revolutionary this theology of the Spirit was. Medieval Roman Catholicism had been an essentially impersonal system of salvation. Grace was a "thing" God gave to help sinners along. As a young man, therefore, Luther had never dreamed of actually enjoying direct communion with God. He would make his requests to the saints but never to God himself. But he came to see that communion with God is precisely what the Spirit brings us.

> And besides giving and entrusting to us everything in heaven and on earth, *He has given us His Son and His Holy Spirit in order to bring us to Himself through them.* For, as we explained earlier, we were totally unable to come to a recognition of the Father's favour and grace except through the Lord Christ, who is the mirroring image of the Father's heart. Without Christ we see nothing in God but an angry and terrible Judge. But we could know nothing of Christ either, if it were not revealed to us by the Holy Spirit.[9]

More than any other gift or "thing," by his Spirit God gives us *himself* to know and enjoy. God is the reward of the gospel, and knowing him is the life for which we were made and to which we are saved.

Now if grace was an impersonal thing in medieval Roman Catholicism, so too was faith. Faith was not so much about personal trust in Christ. That would be called "*explicit* faith" and deemed desirable but superfluous to essential require-

---

9. *Luther's Large Catechism*, trans. F. Samuel Janzow (St. Louis, MO: Concordia, 1978), 77 (emphasis added).

ments. After all, it was thought, was it even possible for un-lettered and feeble-minded peasants to grasp the mysteries of the gospel? They could make their way to heaven on the simpler path of "*implicit* faith" (turning up and receiving the sacraments).

For Luther and the Reformers, such "implicit faith" was not true and saving faith. Such "implicit faith" assumed that God would automatically accept and reward church attendance and works of charity: as if God were not concerned with actually knowing us and being known. But in fact, Luther would argue, such works amounted to nothing more than self-dependent idolatry if they did not flow from a personal trust in Christ.

A century later Richard Sibbes (1577–1635), one of the Puritan heirs of the Reformation, would write: "Now of late for these hundred years, in the time of reformation, there hath been more Spirit and more lightsomeness and comfort. Christians have lived and died more comfortably. Why? *Because Christ hath been more known.*"[10]

Note how he phrases it: he does not say "some formula called 'the gospel' hath been more known"; no, "*Christ* hath been more known." Sibbes goes on:

> If we will have the Spirit, study the gospel of Christ. . . . The more Christ is discovered, the more is the Spirit given; and according to the manifestation of Christ what he hath done for us, and what he hath, the more the riches of Christ is unfolded in the church, the more the Spirit goes along with them. The more the free grace and love of God in Christ alone is made known to the church, the more Spirit there is;

---

10. Richard Sibbes, *The Complete Works of Richard Sibbes*, ed. Alexander B. Grosart, 7 vols. (Edinburgh: James Nichol, 1862–1864; repr., Carlisle, PA: Banner of Truth, 1973–1982), 4:215 (emphasis added).

and again back again, the more Spirit the more knowledge of Christ.[11]

And therein is the difference: belief in the Spirit meant that the Reformers did not simply have some slightly alternative message or system; it meant people would personally *know Christ*. Or take how the Heidelberg Catechism couches it when it asks in question 90, "What is the coming-to-life of the new man?" (That is, what does it mean to be born again of the Spirit?) Answer: "It is wholehearted joy in God through Christ and a delight to do every kind of good as God wants us to."[12]

When we consider who the Spirit is, it makes sense that he would be about more than just enabling us to do good works. The Spirit is the one who has eternally enjoyed and empowered the Word as he has gone out from his Father. Through him the Father has eternally expressed his love for his Son, and through him the Son has echoed his Father's love back. When the Father and the Son share their Spirit with us, they share with us *their own life, love, and fellowship*. By the Spirit I experience the new life of being a child of God in Christ; I begin to share the Father's pleasure in the Son and the Son's in the Father; I begin to love as God loves. Jonathan Edwards writes that "the divine principle in the saints is of the nature of the Spirit: for as the nature of the Spirit of God is divine love, so divine love is the nature and essence of that holy principle in the hearts of the saints."[13] This Spirit would not be about anything less. Because of who he is, he must be about planting and growing cordial love for God.

---

11. Ibid., 4.214–15.

12. *Ecumenical Creeds and Reformed Confessions* (Grand Rapids, MI: CRC, 1988), 54.

13. Jonathan Edwards, "Treatise on Grace," in *The Works of Jonathan Edwards*, vol. 21, *Writings on the Trinity, Grace, and Faith*, ed. Sang Hyun Lee (New Haven, CT: Yale University Press, 2003), 191.

None of this has become any less important or any less relevant down through the centuries. Still today Christians display a strong gravitational pull away from knowing God. We can believe (and proclaim) some message called "the gospel," and we can hold a high view of the Bible, go to church, and live what we like to think are "holy(ish)" lives—and *still* not actually know God. Our "gospel" can be a "Get out of hell free" deal we have signed, where knowing Christ is nonessential. Our "holiness" can be nothing more than self-dependent morality. This is precisely what sin does in us: it draws us away from keeping the greatest commandment, that we love the Lord our God (Matt. 22:37). This is precisely why the Reformers' theology of the Spirit is so necessary for the church's health today: it means the difference between that zombie religiosity the West has grown so sick of and a living faith that can transform it.

And surely the Reformation also presents us with a challenge here. Ritualism—the notion that religious practices, by their very performance, bring grace—is not something that has disappeared with the passing years. Christian bookstores, both Catholic and Protestant, groan under the weight of all the how-to guides. And, we feel, why not? When life is so busy, it is temptingly simple to follow a "Five Steps to Better Spiritual Health" manual. If our cars, our computers, and our bodies tick over better when we follow a few essential techniques, why not our spiritual lives and our churches? And, indeed, there *are* many skills and practices that can be enormously beneficial. But there is such a thing as outward performance that is spiritually hollow. I can read my Bible, say my prayers, and be the linchpin of my home group without treasuring Christ. I can preach, pastor, teach, and lead without sincerely turning to him for aid. And so we need the Reformers' theology of the Spirit to help preserve us from such empty formalism.

The Spirit of Adoption

For the Reformers the Spirit not only gives a new heart, a new life, and a new enjoyment of God; he also gives a whole new assurance. In Roman Catholicism there could be no assurance to speak of. Your fate would rest upon your own personal holiness, and it would be idiotically presumptuous to imagine yourself intrinsically worthy of heaven. And that, of course, would affect your motivation in the Christian life: without assurance of your standing with God you could hardly rejoice in him. Your Christian life and service would spring not from an *overflow* of delight and gratitude but from a *need* to secure salvation.

How different it was with the Reformers' view of the Spirit! There comfort and assurance for believers were staples. The word Luther would use most often in his hymns to describe the Holy Spirit was *Tröster* (Comforter). Or take John Calvin as an example. He asks, "How do we receive those benefits which the Father bestowed on his only-begotten Son—not for Christ's own private use, but that he might enrich poor and needy men?" Answer: through "the secret energy of the Spirit, *by which we come to enjoy Christ and all his benefits. . . .* To sum up, the Holy Spirit is the bond by which Christ effectually unites us to himself."[14] In other words, the work of the Spirit—who is the Spirit of adoption—is so to unite us to the Son that we get to share the life *and the assurance* of the Son before God the Father. Calvin continues:

> He is called the "spirit of adoption" because he is the witness to us of the free benevolence of God with which God the Father has embraced us in his beloved only-begotten Son to become a Father to us; and he encourages us to have

---

14. Calvin, *Institutes*, 3.1.1 (emphasis added).

trust in prayer. In fact, he supplies the very words so that we may fearlessly cry, "Abba, Father!" [Rom. 8:15; Gal. 4:6].

For the same reason he is called "the guarantee and seal" of our inheritance [2 Cor. 1:22; compare Eph. 1:14] because from heaven he so gives life to us, on pilgrimage in the world and resembling dead men, as to assure us that our salvation is safe in God's unfailing care.[15]

Embraced by God the Father in his beloved Son, believers are assured by the Spirit "that our salvation is safe in God's unfailing care." For we are no longer slaves, and we are not mere selfs empowered to do good by some force called "the Spirit." The Spirit of adoption has united us to Christ to share his life and secure status. As Calvin puts it, "our salvation *consists* in having God as our Father."[16]

That being the case, Calvin taught that our faith (which he called "the principal work of the Holy Spirit"[17]) is meant to be a certain thing. The Spirit wants the children of God to be assured of the Father's unbreakable love for them. In stark contrast with the Roman Catholic idea of an "implicit faith," here is Calvin's definition of saving faith:

> Now we shall possess a right definition of faith if we call it *a firm and certain knowledge of God's benevolence toward us,* founded upon the truth of the freely given promise in Christ, both *revealed to our minds and sealed upon our hearts through the Holy Spirit.*[18]

For the comfort and joy of God's people the Spirit is given. Then they can rest in him and know with certainty that he is theirs and they are his.

---

15. Calvin, *Institutes*, 3.1.3.
16. Calvin, *Commentary*, on Rom. 8:17 (emphasis added).
17. Calvin, *Institutes*, 3.1.4.
18. Calvin, *Institutes*, 3.2.7 (emphases added).

For the Word of God is not received by faith if it flits about in the top of the brain, but when it takes root in the depth of the heart that it may be an invincible defense to withstand and drive off all the stratagems of temptation. But if it is true that the mind's real understanding is illumination by the Spirit of God, then in such confirmation of the heart his power is much more clearly manifested, to the extent that the heart's distrust is greater than the mind's blindness. It is harder for the heart to be furnished with assurance than for the mind to be endowed with thought. The Spirit accordingly serves as a seal, to seal up in our hearts those very promises the certainty of which it has previously impressed upon our minds; and takes the place of a guarantee to confirm and establish them.[19]

The Spirit's Reformation

Deep heart metamorphosis instead of superficial behavioral change, personal communion with God instead of abstract blessing, and joy-inducing assurance: these were some of the vital benefits of the Reformers' theology of the Spirit.

But in fact the Reformers' view of the Spirit really permeated *everything* they fought for. If he is the giver of life, then salvation must be by *grace alone*. If he, the Spirit of adoption, freely unites us to Christ, salvation is by *faith alone* in *Christ alone*—and must be about knowing God with the security of the Son. In fact Calvin showed that the Spirit even keeps us from placing any other authority over that of Scripture, so protecting the principle of *Scripture alone*. We believe Scripture, he argued, not finally because the church tells us to or because intelligent men persuade us that we can, but because the Spirit opens our eyes and witnesses to us that Scripture is indeed God's own Word.

---

19. Calvin, *Institutes*, 3.2.36.

Even if anyone clears God's Sacred Word from man's evil speaking, he will not at once imprint upon their hearts that certainty which piety requires. Since for unbelieving men religion seems to stand by opinion alone, they, in order not to believe anything foolishly or lightly, both wish and demand rational proof that Moses and the prophets spoke divinely. But I reply: the testimony of the Spirit is more excellent than all reason. For as God alone is a fit witness of himself in his Word, so also the Word will not find acceptance in men's hearts before it is sealed by the inward testimony of the Spirit. . . .

Let this point therefore stand: that those whom the Holy Spirit has inwardly taught truly rest upon Scripture, and that Scripture indeed is self-authenticated. . . . And the certainty it deserves with us, it attains by the testimony of the Spirit.[20]

The fact that the Spirit is found in every doctrine the Reformers fought for should not be surprising. All the life-giving truths of the Reformation are life-giving because they are to do with him, the giver of life. The Reformation was a human movement, but it was also a movement of the Spirit, and that means that if we are to see the church and our world reformed, revitalized, and made healthy, we need him. We need to cry out, in the words of Luther's revealingly Reformational Pentecost hymn:

Come, Holy Ghost, God and Lord!
Be all Thy graces now outpoured
On each believer's mind and heart;
Thy fervent love to them impart.
Lord, by the brightness of Thy light
Thou in the faith dost men unite

---

20. Calvin, *Institutes*, 1.7.4–5.

Of every land and every tongue;
This to Thy praise, O Lord, our God, be sung.
Hallelujah! Hallelujah!

Thou holy Light, Guide divine,
Oh, cause the Word of Life to shine!
Teach us to know our God aright
And call Him Father with delight.
From every error keep us free;
Let none but Christ our Master be
That we in living faith abide,
In Him, our Lord, with all our might confide.
Hallelujah! Hallelujah!

Thou holy Fire, Comfort true,
Grant us the will Thy work to do
And in Thy service to abide;
Let trials turn us not aside.
Lord, by Thy power prepare each heart
And to our weakness strength impart
That bravely here we may contend,
Through life and death to Thee, our Lord, ascend.
Hallelujah! Hallelujah!

8

The Sacraments

Why Do We Take Bread and Wine?

The Reformers did not agree on everything. And the sacraments were the issue on which they disagreed most. Actually that is something of an understatement. As we shall see, Luther and Zwingli had a major falling out over the significance of the Lord's Supper. But this does not mean there was no agreement and no reforming going on with this issue.

Look closely at a British coin and you will find the following text around the Queen's head: "ELIZABETH II D.G. REG. F.D." It stands for "Elizabeth II *Dei Gratia Regina Fidei Defensor*," or "Elizabeth the Second, by the grace of God, Queen and Defender of the Faith."

The British monarch has had the title "Defender of the Faith" ever since October 11, 1521, when Pope Leo X conferred it on Henry VIII. The reason was a book Henry had written entitled *Assertio septem sacramentorum*, "I assert that there are seven sacraments." Within ten years Henry VIII had broken with Rome. So the pope excommunicated him and revoked the title. The British Parliament stepped in and in 1544 reconferred the title on Henry and his successors, whom Parliament now regarded as defenders of the Church of England.

But back in 1521 Henry was firmly on the side of Rome. And what provoked this royal foray into theology was Martin Luther's book *The Babylonian Captivity of the Church*.

Published the previous year, *The Babylonian Captivity* was a major attack on the Roman Catholic view of the sacraments. This was a priority for Luther, because most people's exposure to the Christian faith was not in the form of theological treatises or university debates. It was in the Sunday services of the local church. So, for true change to take place and true faith to be born in people's hearts, the Reformers needed to reform the preaching and worship of the church.

As we mentioned in the last chapter, the Catholic Church believed there were seven sacraments—baptism, confirmation, the Eucharist, penance, the anointing of the sick (including the last rites), holy orders, and matrimony. Luther argued that a sacrament is an outward sign of God's promises for all God's people, so there are only two sacraments—baptism and the Eucharist. The Reformers were not opposed to the other five activities (albeit with some major modifications, particularly rejecting any notion that we could self-atone for sin through acts of penance). But they were opposed to the underlying theology.

According to medieval Catholicism, the bread really became the physical body of Jesus, and the wine really became the physical blood of Jesus. This was known as "transubstantiation." It was said that in the moment of consecration the "substance" (the inner essence) of the elements changed to become the body and blood of Jesus, while the "accidents" (the outward form) of the bread and blood stayed the same. So the bread and wine still looked and tasted like bread and wine. But their inner essence had changed. This meant that Jesus was being offered again in the Supper. In 1215 the Fourth Lateran Council made transubstantiation the official teaching of the Roman Catholic Church.

It remains official Catholic teaching to this day. The contemporary *Catechism of the Catholic Church* says:

> By the consecration the transubstantiation of the bread and wine into the Body and Blood of Christ is brought about. Under the consecrated species of bread and wine Christ himself, living and glorious, is present in a true, real and substantial manner: his Body and his Blood, with his soul and his divinity. (§1413)

On the Supper as a fresh sacrifice of Christ the *Catechism* says, quoting the Council of Trent:

> The Eucharist is also a sacrifice. . . . In the Eucharist Christ gives us the very body which he gave up for us on the cross, the very blood which he "poured out for many for the forgiveness of sins." (§1365)

> "The victim is one and the same: the same now offers through the ministry of priests, who then offered himself on the cross; only the manner of the offering is different." "In this divine sacrifice which is celebrated in the Mass, the same Christ who offered himself once in a bloody manner on the altar of the cross is contained and is offered in an unbloody manner." (§1367)

In Catholicism the Supper became known as "the Mass." The word "Mass" comes from the Latin word *missa*, which means "dismissal." It is a medieval Latin corruption of the word *missio*, the term from which we get our word "mission." It was taken from the closing words of the service: *Ite, missa est,* "Go, it is the dismissal." The gathered congregation was being sent out into the world in mission. But for the Reformers and their descendants the term was forever associated with the distortions of a biblical theology of the sacraments.

It is important to recognize that Catholic sacramental theology reflected and reinforced the medieval Catholic view of sin and salvation. Transubstantiation was not a random addition. Nor was it simply superstition. It was a natural corollary of the Catholic view of salvation. If sin is a disease and salvation is primarily an act of healing, then the sacraments are the medicine. The wafer on the tongue is like a pill. Or, to change the metaphor, going to the Mass is like going to a gas station to get more fuel for the journey.

This is because Catholicism made grace a "thing" you could transfer, as we have seen. It was natural, then, to view the sacraments as the means by which grace was transferred. Being baptized conveyed regenerating power so that you were born again as a Christian. Receiving the bread was like popping another can of Red Bull—spiritual energy to keep you going in your efforts to lead a virtuous life.

Once this view of the sacraments was in place, you did not even need to be present. So people could pay for "votive" Masses performed on their behalf to secure God's favor. And why not extend their effectiveness to the dead? So the wealthy left bequests to ensure that Masses were said on their behalf to secure their speedy release from purgatory. Many medieval parish churches in England had chantry chapels or side chapels to accommodate these Masses. The result, at its worst, was a commercialization of the Lord's Supper. If grace was a thing that could be moved about, then it could be bought and sold. Martin

Luther said, "I regard the preaching and selling of the mass as a sacrifice or good work as the greatest of all abominations."[1]

The Mass was no longer an act performed by the whole congregation, but an act performed on behalf of the church by a priest. Only the bread was given to the laity, for example, for fear they might spill the wine and so profane what was now the physical blood of Jesus. The service was conducted in Latin, a language few could understand. When the priest lifted up the bread, he would say, *Hoc est corpus meum*, the Latin for "This is my body." One theory is that this led to the expression *hocus-pocus*, which we use colloquially for a spell or something bogus. At this moment in the service a bell was rung so people could look at what was now the body of Christ. The feast of Corpus Christi, "the Body of Christ," developed in which the consecrated host was paraded through the streets with people bowing before it.

In *The Babylonian Captivity of the Church* Luther rejects transubstantiation. He believes Jesus is present in the bread, but rejects the rationalistic explanation of this offered in the doctrine of transubstantiation. For Luther it is enough to accept this reality by faith.

Luther also rejects the practice of giving only the bread to the laity. Luther can see no scriptural or historical precedent for this. More importantly it reflects a view of Christian worship in general and the Eucharist in particular as acts performed on behalf of the people. Luther views worship as something in which the church participates together. As a result, he created liturgies in German rather than Latin so people could follow what was happening.

Above all, Luther rejects in *The Babylonian Captivity* the

---

1. *Luther's Works*, 37:370–71.

idea that the priest makes an offering in the Mass which earns merit for the people. This reflects his growing understanding of salvation. We are justified by faith alone. So the Mass cannot be a merit-earning work. It must be something else. Luther argues that it is given by Christ as an aid to faith. We are already justified by Christ. We are already righteousness in him. His work is finished and so does not need extending or topping up in the Mass. Our righteousness is "alien." It is given to us through Christ. It is not something internal that we acquire in the sacraments. For Luther grace is not a "thing" but God's undeserved love to sinners. It is relational. So what we receive in the sacraments is Christ himself. We receive the presence of Christ and the promises of Christ to strengthen our faith.

This still matters. The Supper is a reminder that the sacrifice of Christ is complete. This is the message of Hebrews 10:

> And every priest stands daily at his service, offering repeatedly the same sacrifices, which can never take away sins. But when Christ had offered for all time a single sacrifice for sins, he sat down at the right hand of God, waiting from that time until his enemies should be made a footstool for his feet. For by a single offering he has perfected for all time those who are being sanctified. (10:11–14)

"A single offering . . . for all time." The writer of Hebrews says that God never needed the sacrifices of the Old Testament (10:8). They were not offered for his benefit. What need did God have of dead sheep? Instead they were commanded as visual aids to point to the work of Christ. God did not want sacrifices, because God himself would provide the sacrifice. Now that sacrifice has been made by Christ, there is nothing left that we need to do to win God's approval. We have his approval in Christ.

It is not just religious people who need to hear this message.

My (Tim's) friend Phil attended a seminar for entrepreneurs. Everyone was asked to bring an object that summarized their business. One man brought his wedding ring. His business had led to divorce. In a candid moment he acknowledged that he had sacrificed his marriage for the sake of success. Many people today make huge sacrifices to appease their gods. They worship success, approval, pleasure, identity, security. And their worship may involve sacrificing time, family, and health. Every celebration of the Lord's Supper is a reminder that we worship a God who, like other gods, requires sacrifice, but who, unlike every other god, himself makes the sacrifice.

Luther versus Zwingli

Martin Luther and Huldrych Zwingli fell out badly over the Lord's Supper, as we shall see. But in fact there was much on which they agreed. They both recognized that the Mass was central to Roman Catholic theology, so they could not reform the church without reforming the Mass. They both wanted to reinstitute the Supper as a participatory act performed by the congregation. So they both argued that the wine as well as the bread should be offered to the congregation. They both wanted the service to be conducted in the language of the people. They insisted that the Word should be central to the service, so the sacraments were interpreted by the Word. Above all, they rejected transubstantiation and the reoffering of Christ. The Supper did not replace or repeat the once-for-all sacrifice of Christ.

But a sharp and personal disagreement arose between Luther and Zwingli. Jesus had instituted the Supper with these words:

> And he took bread, and when he had given thanks, he broke it and gave it to them, saying, "This is my body, which is given for you. Do this in remembrance of me."

> And likewise the cup after they had eaten, saying, "This
> cup that is poured out for you is the new covenant in my
> blood." (Luke 22:19–20)

Luther emphasized the words "this is" and "covenant." He called
the Supper a covenant or testament. The words "this is" imply
an objective reality that is presented to us. It is not something we
perform but something we receive as a token of God's covenant.

Luther developed a doctrine of "consubstantiation." The Lutherans rejected the Catholic idea of transubstantiation. But they
argued that the humanity of Jesus was joined to his divinity at
the ascension. As a result his body moved beyond the confines of
space and became ubiquitous (everywhere). In this way the body
of Christ could really be said to be present in the bread and wine.

Zwingli emphasized the words "do this" and "remembrance." He described the Supper as a memorial. The words
"do this" imply something we do to remember what Christ has
done for us. The bread is not literally the body of Christ, but a
reminder of his body given for us.

The word "sacrament" comes from the Latin word for a
military pledge. For Luther the sacraments were the promise or
pledge that God makes to his people in the gospel. For Zwingli
the sacraments were the pledge of allegiance that we make to
God. Perhaps he was influenced by his work as a chaplain in
the Swiss army. Zwingli eventually died in battle, defending the
Swiss cantons from a Catholic army. Just as a soldier pledges allegiance to his army, so the Christian pledges allegiance to God
through the sacraments. So, for Zwingli, preaching is primary
and the sacraments represent our response. He writes:

> If a man sews on a white cross [the symbol of the Swiss
> army now incorporated into the Swiss flag], he proclaims
> that he wishes to be a confederate [a member of the Swiss

Confederation]. . . . Similarly, the man who receives the mark of baptism is the one who is resolved to hear what God says to him, to learn the divine precepts, and to live his life in accordance with them. And the man who in the remembrance or supper gives thanks to God in the congregation testifies to the fact that from the very heart he rejoices in the death of Christ, and thanks him for it.[2]

Luther on the Sacraments	Zwingli on the Sacraments
The seven sacraments of Roman Catholicism are replaced with two—baptism and the Supper.	
The sacraments are participatory acts performed by the congregation in their own language with the laity taking both the bread and wine.	
The Word is central and the sacraments are interpreted by the Word.	
Christ's death is once for all, so the Supper does not involve reoffering Christ or earning merit.	
"This is my body" means Jesus is present in the bread.	"This is my body" means the bread signifies Christ's body.
The body of Jesus is present everywhere and therefore present in the Supper.	The body of Jesus is at God's right hand and therefore absent from the Supper.
Both the Word and the sacraments proclaim the promises of the gospel.	The Word proclaims the gospel and the sacraments express our response.
The sacraments produce faith.	The sacraments express faith.
We baptize infants to give them a promise that may produce saving faith.	We baptize infants to show they belong to the Christian community.
The Word and the Supper are combined in a weekly act of worship.	The Word is central to weekly worship with the Supper celebrated three or four times a year.

2. Huldrych Zwingli, "Of Baptism," cited in Alister McGrath, *Reformation Thought: An Introduction* (Oxford: Blackwell, 1988), 124.

At the Frankfurt Book Fair of 1527 Luther's book *That the Words of Christ Still Stand Firm against Fanatics* and Zwingli's riposte *A Friendly Exegesis Addressed to Martin Luther* were displayed side by side—great news for booksellers, but not such good news for gospel unity. Throughout the 1520s their supporters were engaged in a kind of theological warfare. In 1529 the two sides came together at the Marburg Colloquy. The political leaders of Protestant nations were keen to create a military alliance to face the threat of the Catholic Counter-Reformation. On fourteen major points Luther and Zwingli agreed. But on the fifteenth and final point, the Lord's Supper, they could not be reconciled. As they departed, Zwingli cried out in tears, "There are not people on earth with whom I would rather be at one than the Wittenbergers."[3] But it was not to be.

On the final day, Luther entered the room ahead of Zwingli and secretly chalked on the table the words *Hoc est corpus meum*, "This is my body." He then covered them with a cloth. During the debate Zwingli demanded a Scripture passage to prove Luther's contention that Christ was physically present in the bread. At this point Luther dramatically whipped aside the cloth, revealing the words *Hoc est corpus meum*. "Here is our Scripture passage," Luther declared. "You have not yet taken it from us, as you set out to do; we need no other."

Zwingli, of course, knew that the words were from Luke 22:19. But he understood them to mean that the bread *signifies* the body of Jesus. When Jesus said he was the Vine, no one believed he was literally a vine. In the same way, "This is my body" need not and should not be taken literally. Zwingli pointed out that Jesus is now at the right hand of God so cannot

---

3. Cited in Timothy George, *Theology of the Reformers* (Nashville: Broadman; Leicester: Apollos, 1988), 150.

also be present in the bread. Luther responded by saying "at the right hand of God" was a metaphor for God's rule. In other words, those words should not be taken literally!

Luther responded to Zwingli with an illustration. Suppose I show you a silver rose and ask what it is. You would answer, "It's a rose." You would not say, "It's a piece of silver which signifies a rose." It may not be a natural rose, but it is still a rose. Silver, wooden, and paper roses are still essentially roses, not just signs. Both Luther and Zwingli agreed that the bread was a sign. But Luther believed that the body of Christ was present "in, with, and under" the sign.[4]

Zwingli's key text was John 6:63: "It is the Spirit who gives life; the flesh is no help at all." He believed this meant that life is given directly through the Spirit and not through physical means like the bread and wine. He feared that Luther's emphasis added to salvation by faith. Salvation would become salvation by faith plus physical means. Zwingli said, *Credere est edere*, "To believe is to eat."

Present through the Spirit

John Calvin was half a generation after Luther (Calvin was eight years old in 1517 when Luther produced his ninety-five theses). Their lives overlapped, but we have no evidence they ever met. Calvin developed his own distinctive approach to the Lord's Supper, which in some ways lies between the views of Luther and Zwingli.

Calvin argues that the ubiquity of the ascended Christ in Lutheran theology compromises Christ's continuing humanity. It dissolves, as it were, the humanity of Jesus into his divinity.

---

4. *D. Martin Luthers Werke*, 26:383, trans. in H. G. Haile, *Luther: An Experiment in Biography* (New York: Doubleday, 1980), 126–27, cited in George, *Theology of the Reformers*, 151–52.

It is not a real human body if it is not located in a particular location.

> As we have proved by firm and clear testimonies of Scripture, Christ's body was circumscribed by the measure of a human body. Again, by his ascension into heaven he made it plain that it is not in all places, but when it passes into one, it leaves the previous one.[5]

How can Christ's body be visible in one place (in heaven), asks Calvin, and invisible or hidden in another (in the communion bread)? "Where is the very nature of a body," he asks, "and where its unity?"[6] He talks of "that insane notion . . . that his body was swallowed up by his divinity."[7]

Calvin argues there was no need to take the phrase "This is my body" literally. Like Zwingli he points to other metaphorical language in Scripture. When the Bible says Christ is a rock, we do not conclude that he is a lump of inanimate stone. In the same way, when Jesus says, "This is my body," we should not think of the bread as human flesh. If the bread is literal flesh and the blood literal blood, then, says Calvin, we are left with the absurd idea that Christ's body and blood are separated.[8]

Moreover Christ clearly says he will leave his disciples: "I came from the Father and have come into the world, and now I am leaving the world and going to the Father" (John 16:28). For Calvin it was hard to evade the implication that he is not present! If this is interpreted as meaning Christ changes his state so he becomes present everywhere, asks Calvin, why then does he talk of sending the Holy Spirit as his replacement?[9] And why

---

5. Calvin, *Institutes*, 4.17.30.
6. Calvin, *Institutes*, 4.17.29.
7. Calvin, *Institutes*, 4.17.29.
8. Calvin, *Institutes*, 4.17.18, 4.17.23.
9. Calvin, *Institutes*, 4.17.26.

does the New Testament speak of our waiting for Christ, as it does in Acts 3:21 and Philippians 3:20–21?

But if the body of Christ is absent when we take communion, does that mean we are left with a mere memorial as Zwingli argued? Calvin's answer is an emphatic *no*. We really do encounter Christ in the bread and wine. We really do feast on him so that we are nourished—and not just by having our memories jogged. The ascended Christ may be absent in body, but he is present by the Spirit.

> The sharing in the Lord's body, which, I maintain, is offered to us in the Supper, demands neither a local presence, nor the descent of Christ, nor an infinite extension of His body, nor anything of that sort; for, in view of the fact that the Supper is a heavenly act, there is nothing absurd about saying that Christ remains in heaven and is yet received by us. For the way in which He imparts Himself to us is by the secret power of the Holy Spirit, a power which is able not only to bring together, but also to join together, things which are separated by distance, and by a great distance at that.[10]

In other words, the distance between the ascended Christ and ourselves is collapsed by the Holy Spirit. If this "seems unbelievable," then "let us remember how far the secret power of the Holy Spirit towers above our senses, and how foolish it is to wish to measure his immeasurableness by our measure."[11]

Because the Spirit is the Spirit of Christ, he does not simply substitute for Christ. It is not like a husband who cannot attend a date with his wife, so he sends someone else in his place! The Spirit mediates the presence of Christ himself. As a result,

---

10. John Calvin, *Commentary*, on 1 Cor. 11:24.
11. Calvin, *Institutes*, 4.17.10.

Christ really is present with us in the Supper. And he really does feed our hearts by his presence. "Our souls are fed by the flesh and blood of Christ in the same way that bread and wine keep and sustain physical life."[12] Christ "feeds his people with his own body, the communion of which he bestows upon them by the power of his Spirit."[13]

So the communion meal expresses our union with Christ and reinforces it to our experience. Calvin says:

> The bond of this connection is therefore the Spirit of Christ, with whom we are joined in unity, and is like a channel through which all that Christ himself is and has is conveyed to us. For if we see that the sun, shedding its beams upon the earth, casts its substance in some measure upon it in order to beget, nourish, and give growth to its offspring— why should the radiance of Christ's Spirit be less in order to impart to us the communion of his flesh and blood?[14]

It is not that Christ comes down to us in the Lord's Supper. Rather, by the Spirit, we ascend to be with Christ in the Lord's Supper.[15]

Roman Catholicism talked about the bread as the "host." The word comes from the Latin *hostia*, which means "sacrificial victim." Christ is being offered afresh as a sacrifice. So in Roman Catholicism the host is *on* the table. For Calvin Jesus is the host in the sense of the one who welcomes you to the meal. So the host is not *on* the table but *at* the table. The people who serve are just Christ's way of getting the bread off the table to you. It is Jesus who is giving the bread as a sign of his presence and promise.

---

12. Calvin, *Institutes*, 4.17.10.
13. Calvin, *Institutes*, 4.17.18.
14. Calvin, *Institutes*, 4.17.12.
15. Calvin, *Institutes*, 4.17.31.

Why the Sacraments Still Matter

There are two opposite dangers in how we view the sacraments. First, the Catholic Church says that grace is conveyed through the sacraments *ex opere operato*, "from the work worked." In other words, the sacraments work apart from faith. What you think about Red Bull does not affect the kick it gives you—the fact that you doubt its efficacy does not stop its working. In the same way the Catholics say that what you are thinking during communion does not stop the transubstantiated body of Christ having an impact in your life.

But if sin, salvation, and therefore the sacraments are relational, then we need a different analogy. Suppose my father gives me a present. If I believe he hates me, then I shall see his gift as a face-saving act of duty. As a result it will do nothing to strengthen my relationship with him. Indeed it may make it worse. But if I believe my father loves me, then I shall receive his gift as yet another token or pledge of his love. In this case my faith in my father makes all the difference. Faith matters.

But there is an opposite danger—the danger of correlating the efficacy of communion to how I feel about it. If I am moved by the Supper, then it is effective. If I am unmoved, then it is ineffective. So, in this view, what makes it effective is my experience. What makes it effective is me! In this case the Lord's Supper ceases to be a divine act and becomes a human act, and its power is human power.

We live in a culture where everything is about response and feeling. And our contemporary evangelical culture is deeply imbued with this subjectivism. We need to understand that the gospel is entirely outside us. The gospel is not my response. The gospel describes the objective reality to which I am to respond.

This is why the link made in the Reformation between Word

and sacrament is important for us today. Calvin said, "Let it be regarded as a settled principle that the sacraments have the same office as the Word of God: to offer and set forth Christ to us, and in him the treasures of heavenly grace."[16] Marcus Peter Johnson comments:

> For Calvin, the Lord's Supper is not something other than the gospel. He believed the Supper is an ordained means by which God testifies to us of our salvation in Christ. Why? Because at the centre of his understanding of salvation was the conviction that believers are joined to the living Christ: Christ himself is the offer of the gospel, and in our union with him we enjoy all of his benefits.[17]

Johnson himself adds:

> When the gospel is properly preached, the sacraments make clear to us visibly what has been offered to us audibly; or, to put it another way, the sacraments "exegete" the preached Word just as the Word "exegetes" the sacraments—and Christ is offered and received in both.[18]

Part of our problem, as we have seen, is that we sometimes view preaching as primarily conveying information about Christ rather than conveying the presence of Christ. If that is the case, it is no surprise that we then have a problem with the sacraments since it is not obvious how they convey information—other than as a prompt for remembering what has already been said.

So it is helpful to think of the sacraments as embodied promises. Their validity lies in the One who makes the promises.

---

16. Calvin, *Institutes*, 4.14.17.
17. Marcus Peter Johnson, *One with Christ: An Evangelical Theology of Salvation* (Wheaton, IL: Crossway, 2013), 234–35.
18. Ibid., 218–19.

Consider the parallel with the Word. Change takes place when someone responds to the preached Word with faith. But a lack of faith does not invalidate the preaching. In the same way, change takes place when someone responds to the sacramental word with faith. Faith matters. But a lack of faith does not invalidate the sacrament. The meaning does not reside in my response any more than the meaning of the Bible lies in the reader's response.

When Luther was struggling, he would go into the courtyard and shout (in Latin), "I am a baptized man." There is an objective reality when the sacraments are celebrated in the church. Their meaning is not in my response or feeling. The meaning is the gospel embodied in the sign. But the sign is designed to evoke my response and feeling. So we receive it as a promise from God—as a pledge of his intentions. So baptism and the Lord's Supper are not primarily signs of our subjective experience or faith or response. They are signs that point us to the gospel.

9

The Church

Which Congregation Should I Join?

On June 15, 1520, Martin Luther received a papal bull. But this
was no gift-wrapped bovine. The term comes from the Latin
word *bulla*, which means "seal." A papal bull was a document
with the pontifical seal to authenticate it—an official declaration from Rome. This was not simply the pope's personal opinion. This was a decree of the self-proclaimed "vicar of Christ,"
Christ's representative on earth. The papal bull Luther received
threatened his excommunication. It listed forty-one sentences
drawn from his writings that it called on him to repudiate, giving him sixty days to do so.

Luther burned it. Publicly.

An edict of excommunication duly followed. On January 3, 1521, Luther was officially no longer a member of the
church. No big deal, you may think. We live in an age in which
there are many denominations representing many theological

perspectives. Leaving one congregation simply means choosing another. But in the sixteenth century the Roman Catholic Church was *the* church. You could not go to another church down the road. There was no other church. If you left the church, then you were quite literally on your own. True, there was the Eastern Orthodox Church, from which the Roman Church had split in 1054. But that was away beyond the borders of the empire in the Greek and Slavic states. There was certainly no local Orthodox congregation for Luther to join. And even if there had been, he would have found a similar set of theological problems. In Western Europe the church was the institutional Church of Rome represented by the pope, and that was it. Luther was outside the church.

To make matters worse, the church had always said, "Outside the church there is no salvation." So, it seemed, Luther was now in the place where there was no salvation. A lesser man might well have stepped back at that point. But Luther stepped forward.

A True Church

Luther took the bold step of declaring that the Catholic Church was no longer the true church. To most people at the time this was errant nonsense. Yes, maybe the church could do with some reform. But how could you say it was not the true church? It could trace its history back to Jesus and the apostles. This was the church the apostle Peter himself had founded. This church had a presence in parishes across the known world. If this was not the church, what was?

But Luther said that the church is not defined by its institutional structures, nor by its historical lineage. He disliked the word *Kirche*, the German equivalent of the English word "church," because it had come to have connotations of a building or institution. He preferred *Gemeine* (community) or *Versammlung* (assembly). Once when asked for a definition of the church, Luther replied, "Why, a seven-year-old child knows what the church is, namely, holy believers and sheep who hear the voice of their Shepherd."[1] It is the gospel of Jesus Christ that defines the church. Luther says:

> The sure mark by which the Christian congregation can be recognized is that the pure gospel is preached there. For just as the banner of an army is the sure sign by which one can know what kind of lord and army has taken to the field, so too the gospel is the sure sign by which one knows where Christ and his army are encamped. . . . Likewise, where the gospel is absent and human teachings rule, there no Christians live but only pagans, no matter how numerous they are and how holy and upright their life may be.[2]

Initially the Reformers simply wanted to *reform* the church. They had no intention of founding a new one. They saw themselves as temporally separated from the church for the sake of the church. But as the Reformation continued, it became clear that no reform or reconciliation was going to take place. In 1541, at the Colloquy of Regensburg, the last attempt at compromise between Catholics and Protestants collapsed. The problem was not a moral issue—the Reformers accepted that on earth and in history the church would always have elements of corruption. The issue was theological. Luther had described justification by faith as "the article by which the church stands or falls." Since the medieval Catholic Church was denying justification by faith through its teaching and practice, it was fallen.

---

1. Martin Luther, *Smalcald Articles*, cited in T. G. Tappert, *The Book of Concord* (Philadelphia: Fortress, 1949), 315.
2. *Luther's Works*, 41:231–32.

There was no alternative but to separate from the Catholic Church.

But this appeared to make the Reformers schismatic, and they knew from Augustine that schism was a terrible sin. They could uphold Augustine's doctrine of grace, it seemed, only by denying his doctrine of the church. But defining the church as that body which preached the Word allowed Luther to reconcile these apparently opposing truths. It was not the Reformers who had departed from the true church. It was Rome that had departed from the true gospel. John Calvin developed this further:

> Wherever we see the Word of God preached purely and heard, and the sacraments administered according to Christ's institution, there, it is not to be doubted, a church of God exists. . . .
>
> . . . If it has the ministry of the Word and honors it, if it has the administration of the sacraments, it deserves without doubt to be held and considered a church.[3]

The marks of a true church are twofold: the gospel and the sacraments. In other words, a true church is one that both faithfully proclaims the gospel word from the Scriptures and faithfully administers the gospel sacraments of baptism and communion. The implication is that a church which no longer proclaims the true gospel of grace under the authority of Scripture is not a true church.

So, while Calvin shares Augustine's concern for unity, he adds an important qualification: "For the Lord esteems the communion of his church so highly that he counts as a traitor and apostate from Christianity anyone who arrogantly leaves any Christian society, provided it cherishes the true ministry

---

3. Calvin, *Institutes*, 4.1.9.

of the Word and sacraments."[4] This is precisely the accusation Catholics made against the Reformers—that they were "apostates" who had "arrogantly" left the church. But you are an apostate, says Calvin, only if you leave a church that "cherishes the true ministry of the Word and sacraments."

The Roman Catholic Church openly repudiated the gospel of justification by faith, so it could no longer be considered a true church.[5] The Reformers were not schismatic. They had not left the true church. They had made the break with Rome to *continue* the true church. A true church is formed *by* the preaching of the gospel *for* the preaching of the gospel. The Catholic Church said the true church existed wherever the authority of the pope held sway. The Reformers said the true church existed wherever the authority of the gospel held sway.

The Catholic Church claimed there is no salvation outside the church. The Reformers agreed with this claim. The church is the people for whom Christ died and who have found salvation in his name. To be saved is to be part of this people. But the church, argued the Reformers, is not to be equated with an institution based in Rome. The church is the universal body of people on earth and in heaven who have been formed by the gospel. You are not saved by being part of the church. You are part of the church by being saved.

Before coming to Geneva in 1541 Calvin spent three years in Strasbourg, where the leading Reformer was Martin Bucer. From Bucer Calvin learned to make a distinction between the visible and the invisible church. The invisible church consists of all true Christians. The visible church is the institution on earth and its congregations. The visible church includes both true believers and false. Luther had spoken of the *ecclesiola in ecclesia*,

---

4. Calvin, *Institutes*, 4.1.10.
5. Calvin, *Institutes*, 4.2.

"the little church within the church." There is only one invisible church with Christ as its head, even if it is visible in different congregations (and even in different denominations). In other words, the invisible church is one even if the visible church is not. In history the church appears disunited. It is tainted by sin and corruption. But at the climax of history the unity of the church will be revealed. It will be seen that the invisible church has been one throughout the ages. In the meantime believers should be committed to the visible church in all its weaknesses for the sake of the invisible church.

This distinction between the visible and the invisible church enabled Calvin to live with the ambiguities of people in a congregation who were not true believers. He cites the example of the congregations to whom Paul wrote. They were sometimes full of problems and scandals, but Paul still wrote to them *as churches*. So Calvin warns against leaving a church simply because it is tainted with sin.[6] There is little doubt that Calvin has in mind, at least in part, the Anabaptists.

A Gathered Church

The Anabaptists had their origins in Zurich. Conrad Grebel, the son of a city councillor, became one of the pupils of Zwingli, Zurich's leading Reformer. Originally the plan was to study the Greek language. But when Zwingli introduced Grebel and his companions to the Greek New Testament, they became captivated by its message. Grebel's radicalism soon exceeded that of Zwingli, and a dispute arose between them. It ended up before the city council, which ruled in favor of Zwingli. Grebel was given three options: submit to Zwingli, leave the city, or be imprisoned. He chose prison. The sentence,

---

6. Calvin, *Institutes*, 4.1.14–15.

however, was delayed. And that allowed time for a momentous act. On January 21, 1525, a group of about twelve men met in the home of a man called Felix Manz. A former priest named George Blaurock was baptized by Grebel. Then Blaurock baptized the remaining members of the group. The Baptist movement was born.

Melchior Hofmann was an Anabaptist church planter in Germany and Holland who died in prison for his beliefs. In 1530 he wrote a treatise on baptism entitled *The Ordinance of God*.[7] Hofmann begins with the Great Commission and Christ's command to proclaim the gospel to all nations. We are to urge people, he says, to "wed and bind themselves to the Lord Jesus Christ, publicly, through the true sign of the Covenant, the water bath and baptism."[8] Throughout the treatise Hofmann likens baptism to a wedding ceremony, and communion to a wedding feast. Converts "betroth themselves to [Jesus Christ] through the covenant of baptism and also give themselves over to him dead and crucified and hence are at all times subject, in utter zeal, to his will and pleasure."[9] Having become, both individually and collectively, the bride of Christ through baptism, Christians now live in covenant fidelity.

Because baptism expresses this marriage-like commitment, it is only for those who can make such a commitment. The covenant sign is for

> the old, the mature, and the rational, who can receive, assimilate, and understand the teaching and the preaching of the Lord, and not for the immature, uncomprehending, and

---

7. Melchior Hofmann, "The Ordinance of God" (1530), in *Spiritual and Anabaptist Writers*, ed. George H. Williams and Angel M. Mergal, Library of Christian Classics 25 (London: SCM; Philadelphia: Westminster, 1957), 182–203.
8. Ibid., 186–87.
9. Ibid., 187.

unreasonable, who cannot receive, learn, or understand the teaching of the apostolic emissaries.[10]

By "immature, uncomprehending, and unreasonable" Hofmann specifically has in mind "immature children." There are no examples of the New Testament apostles ever baptizing an infant, he says, "nor will any such instance be found in all eternity!"[11] For we are commanded to baptize "those who accept their word and preachment of the crucified Christ Jesus and give themselves over to him of their own free will."[12] Hofmann left little room for compromise:

> Paedobaptism is absolutely not from God but rather is practiced, out of wilfulness, by anti-Christians and the satanic crowd, in opposition to God and all his commandments, will, and desire. Verily, it is an eternal abomination to him. Woe, woe to all such blind leaders.[13]

The Reformation led by Martin Luther and John Calvin—what became the Lutheran, Reformed, and Anglican churches—is often known as the "Magisterial Reformation." This is because they appealed to the magistrates—the secular authorities—to promote and defend the Protestant faith. Their works were often addressed to princes and nobles because they wanted to persuade those in power to create a Protestant nation or city. In other words, they continued to operate with a state-church model. The state and church were still tied together in a mutually supportive relationship. Zwingli, for example, would die in battle while leading a Protestant army against Catholic armies. In this model you were part of the visible church because of where you were born.

This understanding of the church was challenged by the

---

10. Ibid., 192.
11. Ibid.
12. Ibid., 193.
13. Ibid., 196.

Anabaptists or "radical Reformation." They were called "*Ana-baptists*" because they *re*baptized people. Of course, they did not see themselves as rebaptizers. They believed infant baptism was invalid. So when they baptized professing believers, they saw this not as a rebaptism, but as a first, true baptism. But the underlying issue was not simply baptism. It had to do with how one understands the church.

Some Anabaptists became fanatical, with an emphasis on hearing the Spirit independently of Scripture. Most famously a group led by Jan of Leiden, consumed with apocalyptic urgency, took the city of Münster with violence to proclaim a New Jerusalem. All the godless, which meant those who refused to be baptized, were to be killed. Jan then styled himself a new King David and introduced polygamy. Three times a week he would appear in the market square to receive expressions of obedience from his people. This New Jerusalem ended in a bloodbath when the city was overrun by an army of Protestant and Catholic troops, for once fighting together. Jan was tortured to death, and his body hung in an iron cage in the main street. The iron cage is there to this day.

This extremism provided plenty of fuel for anti-Anabaptist propaganda. The Magisterial Reformers routinely lumped all the Anabaptists together, which allowed them to reject their arguments with dark allusions to fanaticism. Luther referred to them as *Schwärmer*, which means "dreamers" or "enthusiasts," but also has the connotation of swarming bees. Calvin variously called them "fanatics," "deluded," "scatter brains," "asses," "scoundrels" and "mad dogs."[14] Still to this day this is how Anabaptists are often portrayed.

---

14. John Calvin, *Treatises against the Anabaptists and against the Libertines*, ed. Benjamin W. Farley (Grand Rapids, MI: Baker, 1982), 30, cited in Timothy George, *Theology of the Reformers* (Nashville: Broadman; Leicester: Apollos, 1988), 252.

But such fanaticism was far from universal. Many were pacifists, a legacy that continues to this day in the Mennonite tradition. Others practiced a community of goods. Those sometimes known as the "evangelical Anabaptists" were as committed to the authority of Scripture as any of the Magisterial Reformers. Indeed they believed they were more committed to Scripture because they were prepared to use Scripture to rethink the nature of the church.

The Radical Reformation saw the church as a "gathered community." It consisted of believers gathered from the world into a community of faith. One of the leading figures in the movement was Menno Simons (1496–1561), a former Catholic priest from the Netherlands. He spent much of his life on the run, preaching to secret communities by night and baptizing converts in country lakes. Simons said:

> They truly are not the true congregation of Christ who merely boast of his name. But they are the true congregation of Christ who are truly converted, who are born from above of God, who are of a regenerate mind by the operation of the Holy Spirit through the hearing of the divine Word, and have become the children of God, have entered into obedience to him, and live unblamably in his holy commandments, and according to his holy will with all their days, or from the moment of their call.[15]

In other words, you become a member of the church through new birth rather than through birth. Membership of the visible church as well as membership of the invisible church were through faith. The visible church was a gathering of believers. The church was the assembly of believers. Believers' baptism

---

15. Menno Simons, *The Complete Writings of Menno Simons*, ed. John C. Wenger (Scottdale, PA: Herald, 1956), 300.

was simply an outworking of this understanding of the church as a gathered community.

The Anabaptists believed the Magisterial Reformers hid behind the notion of the invisible church, allowing them to live with compromise. For the Anabaptists the church is the visible, concrete brotherhood of believers. This is the kingdom of Christ on earth, the place where he reigns through his Word. So there is a sharp distinction between the world and the church. One is a community of unbelief; the other, of faith.

Baptism represented a radical commitment to follow Jesus within a community of disciples. Simons believed that salvation is by faith alone. But, like a living tree producing fruit, living faith always results in the fruit of a changed life. The church is a community of people whose lives are being transformed by the gospel.

This high view of the local church meant the church needed to take discipleship seriously. People who proved not to be true believers needed to be removed from the church. They had shown themselves not to be part of the true church. Their continuing presence threatened the church's witness and the spiritual walk of its members. Anabaptists were sometimes known as *Catharer*, which means "the pure." But that was not a compliment. "Purists" might be a modern equivalent, with connotations of unrealistic and obsessive idealism. Anabaptists knew the visible church would never be perfect before the return of Christ. But they felt it was the duty of the church to be as holy as possible, just as it is the duty of individual believers to be as holy as possible. The church is to be a countercultural community that witnesses to the world of the coming kingdom of God.

Like the Anabaptists, the Magisterial Reformers believed that the true church (what they called "the invisible church") is the community of people saved by the gospel. And like the Magisterial Reformers the Anabaptists acknowledged that the church on earth and in history will always be marred by sin. So there was significant overlap in their positions. But we should not minimize the differences. These differences resulted in vicious persecution of Anabaptists, some of whom were drowned in a cruel parody of their convictions.

The Magisterial Reformers offered baptism to everyone in the visible church. Indeed there was an expectation that everyone in Protestant states would be baptized as infants. This cooperation of church and state flowed in both directions, with Christian involvement in the city council. Anabaptists offered baptism only to those professing faith and, if that profession proved false, would exclude people from the visible church. The church was to be made up of true believers. The visible church should make every attempt to mirror the invisible church. With this stark polarity between church and state came a reluctance by some Anabaptists (though not all) to play any part in civic institutions. Of course, the routine persecution of Anabaptists by the state did little to encourage their involvement in political matters. Anabaptists soon developed a strong martyr mentality.

Why the Church Still Matters

What would the Reformers say to us today about the church? Of course, we cannot be sure. But they might well marvel at how fickle we are, how quick to switch congregations. They did not leave the Catholic Church willingly or in haste. They did leave and sometimes so must we. But they did so reluctantly and only because the truth of the gospel itself was at stake. Calvin said: "Separation from the church is the denial of God and Christ. . . . Nor can any more atrocious crime be conceived than for us by sacrilegious disloyalty to violate the marriage that the only-begotten Son of God deigned to contract with us."[16] He often spoke of the church as our mother. Mother Church gives us birth and nurtures us through the preaching of the gospel and administration of the sacraments. It is the place where Christians are birthed and grow into maturity.

Nor would the Reformers have been impressed with the loose affiliations or online presence that people sometimes claim as radical expressions of church. The marks of the church include not only the gospel word but also the gospel sacraments. And those embodied acts require an embodied community. They bind us to specific people in specific locations.

Luther, perhaps, would remind us that Christians are "always righteous, always sinful." We rightly celebrate the "always righteous." But sometimes we also need to remember the "always sinful." The church is not a perfect institution full of perfect people. Calvin would, perhaps, remind us that the visible church is not the same as the invisible church. The church in history has many faults but remains connected to the glorious church above. Life in any local church requires patience, forbearance, and grace. The forgiveness we extend to one another in our failings is as much a testimony to the grace of the gospel as our goodness. As the old ditty goes:

To dwell above
with saints we love
will be eternal glory.
To dwell below

---

16. Calvin, *Institutes*, 4.1.10.

with saints we know,
well, that's another story!

Calvin might also remind us that his marks of the church were intended not only to exclude those who did not preach the gospel, but also to embrace all who did. "The principle extends to the point that we must not reject [any church] so long as it retains them, even if it otherwise swarms with many faults."[17] Think of the typical reasons why people leave churches today or churches refuse to cooperate. Calvin continues, "How dangerous—nay, how deadly—a temptation it is, when one is prompted to withdraw from that congregation wherein are seen the signs and tokens with which the Lord thought his church sufficiently marked!"[18] He specifically warns against separating over "nonessential matters."[19]

Nevertheless, the Reformers did leave the Catholic Church. We live today in a time of doctrinal flux. Many congregations and whole denominations are influenced more by the culture than by the Bible. For the Reformers the marks of the church—the gospel word and the gospel sacraments—were an indicator of when one should leave a church. The Reformers would also have encouraged us to see the marks as criteria to determine which church we should join. In other words, the key factor when deciding which church to join is not the style of worship or provision for children or charisma of its leaders, but the gospel. Is this church committed to the Word of God?

Why Church Discipline Still Matters

Calvin and the Anabaptists would also, perhaps, marvel at our neglect of church discipline. Calvin says, "[Christ] so esteems

---

17. Calvin, *Institutes*, 4.1.12.
18. Calvin, *Institutes*, 4.1.11.
19. Calvin, *Institutes*, 4.1.12.

the authority of the church that when it is violated he believes his own diminished."[20] If the gospel is the soul of the church, says Calvin, then discipline is its sinews. If you avoid church discipline, then the body will fall apart. The Word of God must be preached publicly. But this is not enough. A church also needs "private admonitions, corrections, and other aids of the sort that sustain doctrine and do not let it remain idle."[21]

While Calvin emphasizes the importance of gentleness and restraint in church discipline,[22] he is clear that discipline is vital for the following three reasons.[23] First, to avoid bringing dishonor to the name of God: "Since the church itself is the body of Christ, it cannot be corrupted by such foul and decaying members without some disgrace falling upon its Head." Second, to avoid other Christians becoming corrupted: "There is nothing easier than for us to be led away by bad examples from right living." Third, to bring the person concerned to a state of repentance (citing 1 Cor. 5:5; 2 Thess. 3:14).

Pierre Viret (1511–1571), a friend of Calvin and the leading Reformer in Lausanne, was known as "the Smile of the Reformation" because of the warmth of his preaching. Viret wrote an exposition of the Christian faith in the form of a dialogue between two characters, Peter and Nathaniel. Here are Peter and Nathaniel discussing church discipline:

PETER: Do you think we act in mercy if, after a wolf has eaten the sheep, we have pity and compassion on him, and save him that he might eat still others?

NATHANIEL: It seems to me that this would rather be a great cruelty. For this would be to murder the sheep to

---

20. Calvin, *Institutes*, 4.1.10.
21. Calvin, *Institutes*, 4.12.1.
22. Calvin, *Institutes*, 4.12.8–11.
23. Calvin, *Institutes*, 4.12.5.

save the wolves, and abuse the mercy which it is fitting to exercise toward the sheep.

PETER: . . . There are many who, in matters of justice, employ such love and forgiveness, in tolerating the wicked who deserve punishment, and leaving them to trample the righteous and innocent, instead of punishing them as they ought. The same also oft times happens in the Church, when we tolerate far too much the scandalous, and pay no heed to the great damage they bring to the entire Church.[24]

The Anabaptists went further. Despite Calvin's emphasis on the importance of church discipline, he was reluctant to make it a mark of the church. But the Anabaptists believed it was essential. So, while the Magisterial Reformers identified two marks of the church (the Word of God and the sacraments), the Anabaptists made church discipline a third mark. Ultimately this could take the form of excommunication (what they called "the ban"), but it also embraces what we think of as "discipleship." In a true church there is a commitment to discipling one another so that the church may be a light to the world.

Having likened baptism to a wedding, Melchior Hofmann says that the "many brides are become one congregation and bride of the Lord."[25] And, just as would be the case in a human marriage, if there is adultery, then action must be taken. The bride must be kept pure for her husband. This is the basis for church discipline. "Likewise the [heavenly] Bridegroom, through his apostolic emissaries, would thereupon let her be thrown out of the congregation . . . and would divorce her from his fellowship and would take from her the bread and wine."[26]

---

24. Pierre Viret, *Instruction Chrétienne en la doctrine de la loi et de l'Évangile*, vol. 1 (Geneva, 1564; repr., Lausanne: L'Age d'Homme, 2004), 91; accessed October 6, 2015, www.pierreviret.org/theology-ecclesiology.php.
25. Hofmann, "Ordinance of God," 196.
26. Ibid.

The Anabaptists took seriously the three steps outlined by Christ in Matthew 18:15–20. Jesus says, "If your brother sins against you, go and tell him his fault, between you and him alone. If he listens to you, you have gained your brother." That is step one. If, however, the brother refuses to listen, then take a companion. That is step two. The third step is to bring the issue to the church. If the brother still refuses to repent, then "let him be to you as a Gentile and a tax collector." The mandate of Jesus was strong and clear: "Truly, I say to you, whatever you bind on earth shall be bound in heaven, and whatever you loose on earth shall be loosed in heaven." What drove this commitment to church discipline was a commitment to the church as a gathered community of believers, together as a witness to the gospel.

This view of the church and church discipline clashes today with the all-pervasive cult of the individual. The highest value of our age is personal freedom—I am free to determine what is true. The truth is anything I want it to be. My feelings are king. In this context any attempt at church discipline is seen as authoritarian, intrusive, and arrogant. It is seen as a crime against the Self. My own Self is assumed to be all-knowing and all-powerful.

Suppose as a pastor I challenge the thinking or behavior or feelings of members of my church. The New Testament suggests they should weigh my intervention carefully. They have every right—and indeed duty—to test what I say against the authority of Scripture. But they should do so with openness and humility. One of the reasons God has given us the Christian community is so that it might be a context of discipleship. The New Testament calls on us to encourage, rebuke, admonish, and exhort one another.

But in our current cultural climate people often react

aggressively to any challenge. People view it as an assault because it contravenes the personal freedom that is the core conviction of our culture. They quickly reject what is said. It is not simply a question of the rightness or wrongness of the intervention. The very basis of the intervention—that Christians share a common life and live in mutual responsibility—is not accepted. We conform instead to the pattern of this world.

Or people portray themselves as victims. It is striking how quickly the all-competent Self crumples in the face of a challenge to hide behind the mask of victimhood. People do not dispute what is said. Instead they portray themselves as fragile souls who have just been unnecessarily assaulted by your accusations. What they need, they suppose, is people boosting their self-esteem with empty praise—not someone pointing out their faults. Your challenge is another burden they must now carry. The gospel is another demand rather than gracious news that liberates us from our self-obsessions. Victimhood becomes another way of protecting the Self from turning from itself out toward God and others in love.

Do not mistake what we are saying. We are not advocating harsh, uncaring nit-picking. Nor are we advocating authoritarian, top-down dictates. It is undoubtedly true that church discipline can be exercised in a harsh or legalistic manner. But its abuses do not invalidate the biblical mandate. Menno Simons said that Christians should exchange common greetings with those who have been disciplined because "mildness, politeness, respectfulness and friendliness to all mankind becomes all Christians" and we should "not deny necessary service, love, and mercy to the banned" when they are in need.[27] The aim is

---

27. Menno Simons, "A Clear Account of Excommunication" (1550), in Wenger, *Complete Writings of Menno Simons*, 479, 480.

always restoration. In *A Kind Admonition on Church Discipline* Simons wrote:

> No one is excommunicated or expelled by us from the communion of the brethren but those who have already separated and expelled themselves from Christ's communion either by false doctrine or improper conduct. For we do not want to expel any, but rather to receive; not to amputate, but rather to heal; not to discard, but rather to win back; not to grieve, but rather to comfort; not to condemn, but rather to save.[28]

This is a challenging vision in our cultural climate. But we need churches that, inspired by a gospel vision of the church, are prepared to defy the prevailing culture. We need churches committed to being communities of grace in which everyone is "speaking the truth in love" to one another (Eph. 4:15). We need churches that are growing together as the gospel is spoken in the context of everyday life. We need churches where, in Calvin's words, "private admonitions" mean that the Word of God does not "remain idle."[29]

---

28. Menno Simons, "A Kind Admonition on Church Discipline" (1541), in Wenger, *Complete Writings of Menno Simons*, 413.

29. Calvin, *Institutes*, 4.12.1.

10

Everyday Life

What Difference Does God Make
on Monday Mornings?

Soli Deo gloria, "glory to God alone," was one of the key summaries of Reformation thought. The Reformation pushed all the achievement of salvation away from humanity and laid it at the feet of God. No one can say, "I've received eternal life because of my good life or religious devotion or my clever reasoning." All the glory is God's. In this the Reformers were reflecting the thought of Paul in 1 Corinthians 1:28–31:

> God chose what is low and despised in the world, even things that are not, to bring to nothing things that are, so that no human being might boast in the presence of God. And because of him you are in Christ Jesus, who became to us wisdom from God, righteousness and sanctification

and redemption, so that, as it is written, "Let the one who boasts, boast in the Lord."

But *soli Deo gloria* also became a summary of a Reformation *life*. Everyday life became the context in which we glorify God. This emphasis on everyday life stemmed from the Reformers' rediscovery of the Scriptures, for it reflects biblical Christianity. But it also flowed from their rediscovery of justification by faith.

Good Works Redirected

The Mass had come to be regarded as a sacrifice, a reenactment of Calvary that secured the blessing of God. Since this secured God's blessing, then the more it was done, the more pleased God was. And it was not necessary for the congregation to be present. The Mass could be said by clergy repeatedly in a mechanical way. This practice reinforces the idea that the essence of Christianity takes place away from day-to-day life. It leads to a divided world: the spiritual and the secular.

Where does the activity that counts to God take place? If we are justified by infusions of "grace" administered through the sacraments, as the Catholic Church suggested, then the activities that matter are the sacramental activities in the church. Or if we are to achieve union with Christ through mysticism and contemplation, then the activities that matter take place in a monastery. If you are keen on knowing God, then you become a monk. If you are keen on serving God, then you become a priest or friar.

Luther's rediscovery of justification by faith swept away the impetus for such activities. God did not require religious duties as a kind of payment toward salvation. If justification is through faith, then the focus and nature of religious activity shifts radically.

Luther discusses the nature of good works at length in his treatise *The Freedom of a Christian.*[1] And he starts with justification. We are saved by faith alone, and "this faith cannot exist in connection with works."[2] What Luther means is that you cannot claim to be saved partially by faith and partially by works. Any claim that your works contribute to your salvation negates the effectiveness of faith. If faith in Christ alone saves, then nothing else can benefit us.

This raises a question: Why, then, are so many works prescribed in Scripture? One answer is that the commandments of Scripture reveal our helplessness to us. Through them a man is "truly humbled and reduced to nothing in his own eyes."[3] Their purpose is to direct us to the promises of Scripture. They drive us into the arms of Christ.

So can we now neglect good works? Paul's answer to this question in Romans 6:1–2 is "By no means!" And Luther's answer is similar: "I answer: not so, you wicked men, not so." He explains:

> Although, as I have said, a man is abundantly and sufficiently justified by faith inwardly, in his spirit, and so has all that he needs, except insofar as this faith and these riches must grow from day to day even to the future life; yet he remains in this mortal life on earth. In this life he must control his own body and have dealings with men. Here the works begin; here a man cannot enjoy leisure; here he must indeed take care to discipline his body by fasting, watching, labours, and other reasonable discipline and to subject it to the Spirit so that it will obey and conform to the inner man and faith and not revolt against faith and

---

1. Martin Luther, "The Freedom of a Christian," in *Selected Writings of Martin Luther*, vol. 2, *1520–1523*, ed. Theodore G. Tappert (Minneapolis: Fortress, 2007).
2. Ibid., 22.
3. Ibid., 24.

hinder the inner man, as it is the nature of the body to do if it is not held in check. The inner man, who by faith is created in the image of God, is both joyful and happy because of Christ in whom so many benefits are conferred upon him; and therefore it is his one occupation to serve God joyfully and without thought of gain, in love that is not constrained.[4]

Here is what Luther is saying. First, while we do not have to control our bodies so we can attain heaven, we do still have to live "this mortal life on earth," and spiritual disciplines are important to ensure that our outer lives conform to our new inner status so that our body "will obey and conform to the inner man and faith." The extent to which, and the situations in which, each of us needs to fast and labor will vary from person to person because our aim is to control the lusts of the flesh. Such self-disciplines are not an end in themselves but a means to self-control. "But those who presume to be justified by works do not regard the mortifying of the lusts, but only the works themselves, and think that if only they have done as many and as great works as are possible, they have done well and have become righteous."[5]

Second, while we do not have to control our bodies so that we can attain heaven, such is our joy because of the benefits conferred on us in Christ that we now want to "serve God joyfully." Previously we served God because we thought it would lead to our salvation—it was a self-centered service. Now we serve with "love that is not constrained."

Luther then provides a variety of analogies to illustrate his point:

---

4. Ibid., 34–35.
5. Ibid., 35–36.

- We are like pre-fallen Adam and Eve, who worked freely to please God and not to obtain righteousness, which they already had in full measure.
- We are like a bishop who performs his duties because he is a bishop, and not in order to become one.
- We are like a tree that bears good fruit because it is a good tree, and not in order to become a good tree.
- We are like a well-built house. A good house does not make a good builder. It is a good builder who makes a good house. Our works do not make us good. We, once we are made good by faith, then produce good works.

By freeing us from the need for good works for our own salvation, the gospel frees us to do good for the sake of others:

Man . . . needs none of these things for his righteousness and salvation. Therefore he should be guided in all his works by this thought and contemplate this one thing alone, that he may serve and benefit others in all that he does, considering nothing except the need and the advantage of his neighbour.[6]

Instead of *doing* good *for* God, we *have* good *from* God. But this good from God is then meant to flow to others. Christ identified with us so that "from Christ the good things have flowed and are flowing into us." In the same way we are to identify with others so that the good things "flow on to those who have need of them."[7]

The Catholic Church believed that a person did good works to be saved. So good works are done for God, to earn his approval. But Luther rejected the idea that good works are done for God. After all, God has no need of our good works. He is

---

6. Ibid., 41.
7. Ibid., 47.

not in need. Instead our good works are done for our neighbor. So, instead of good works done for God, which take us out of the world (spiritual exercises, monastic life, vows of celibacy and poverty), the gospel drives us back *into the world* to serve others in love.

> We conclude, therefore, that a Christian lives not in himself, but in Christ and in his neighbour. Otherwise he is not a Christian. He lives in Christ through faith, in his neighbour through love. By faith he is caught up beyond himself into God. By love he descends beneath himself into his neighbour.[8]

So where was the best place to do those good works? Not in a monastery or a nunnery. At best the medieval monasteries had been centers for health care, education, and provision for the needy. But too often they had become a retreat from the world into a private world of self-serving prayer and contemplation. They had become the last place where you could serve your needy neighbor, because your needy neighbor was outside.

What makes something a good deed, a deed that pleases God? Medieval Catholicism could list good deeds: the sacraments and so on. However, according to the Reformers it was not the external form of an act that made it good but the faith in which it was conducted. Faith was what pleased God.

This had radical implications for how one viewed life. In the medieval Catholic world changing a nappy could never be understood as a good or spiritual act. Meritorious acts took place in churches and monasteries. But if faith was the determining factor, then any deed could please God if done for him as an

---

8. Ibid., 47.

act of faith. Suddenly the context in which one could serve God had widened from the cloister and the cell to the world. The workshop and hearth were sacred places.

Luther put these convictions into practice in the most concrete ways. In 1523 a group of nuns from the Cistercian convent in Nimbschen contacted Luther. They had become persuaded by the theology of the Reformation, and now they wanted Luther to help them escape their cloistered life. Luther enlisted the cooperation of a merchant who regularly delivered herring to the convent. On April 4 the nuns escaped by hiding among the empty fish barrels. Their families refused to take them back, perhaps because what had just happened was still a crime under church law. So Luther gradually arranged husbands for them all. All except one. No husband could be found for the ringleader, Katharina von Bora. So, somewhat against his wishes, Luther himself married her. He was forty-one and she twenty-six.

Although marriage had not been on Luther's agenda, they proved to be a good match, and a strong affection grew between them. They moved into "the Black Cloister," the old Augustinian monastery where Katharina managed the farm, brewed beer, ran a hospital, entertained students and guests, and bore six children. Luther called her the "morning star of Wittenberg," because she got up at 4:00 a.m. each day, and the "boss of Zulsdorf," the name of the farm.

Priesthood Redefined

Justification by faith meant you no longer needed a priest as an intermediary. All Christians have direct access to God through Christ. So in his 1523 treatise *Concerning the Ministry* Luther argues that every Christian is a priest.[9] Or rather there is only one Priest, Jesus Christ. But all those who are in him are priests with access to God. "We are priests as he is Priest, sons as he is Son, kings as he is King."[10]

The Catholic Church divided itself into two classes: clergy and laity. Luther abolished this distinction. A Christian becomes a priest at his or her baptism. Luther points out that priests in the Old Testament were not appointed but born. Only those belonging to the priestly family could be priests. The same, he argues, is true in the New Testament. We become priests when we are born again. So "all Christians are priests, and all priests are Christians."[11] This means that those of the Catholic hierarchy "make no one a priest until he denies that he was a priest before. Thus in the very act of making him a priest they in fact remove him from his priesthood."[12]

Luther lists seven priestly duties: "Mostly the functions of a priest are these: to teach, to preach and proclaim the Word of God, to baptize, to consecrate or administer the Eucharist, to bind and loose sins, to pray for others, to sacrifice, and to judge of all doctrine and spirits."[13] Luther then works through them one by one and in each case shows they are duties that belong to all Christians. To prevent disorder among God's people, churches will normally choose a few people to lead in these matters, but "in time of emergency each may use it as he deems best."[14] So Luther thinks we should drop the term "priest" for those given responsibility for the Word and sacraments. He concludes:

9. *Luther's Works*, vol. 40.
10. *Luther's Works*, 40:20.
11. *Luther's Works*, 40:19.
12. *Luther's Works*, 40:20.
13. *Luther's Works*, 40:21.
14. *Luther's Works*, 40:34.

Here we take our stand: There is no other Word of God than that which is given all Christians to proclaim. There is no other baptism than the one which any Christian can bestow. There is no other remembrance of the Lord's Supper than that which any Christian can observe and which Christ has instituted. There is no other kind of sin than that which any Christian can bind or loose. There is no other sacrifice than of the body of every Christian. No one but a Christian can pray. No one but a Christian may judge of doctrine. These make the priestly and royal office.[15]

The priesthood of all believers is often misunderstood to mean that there are no offices in the church or that every individual is his or her own priest, accountable to no one else. But for Luther the priesthood of all believers is never about being alone. It is always about being together as a united church. It is a responsibility as well as a privilege, a service as well as a status. God has made us one body, or, using an image Luther was fond of, "one cake," and our unity is displayed in our mutual love. Luther describes the church as *communio sanctorum*, "a community of saints."

The Catholic Church described becoming a priest as "taking holy orders." It still does. Luther co-opted this language and subverted it. "The true holy orders and pious foundations established by God are these three: the priestly office, the family and the civil government."[16] By priestly office he means "those who are engaged in the pastoral office or the ministry of the Word." But it is not just church leaders who take holy orders. Fathers, mothers, children, servants, princes, judges, officials,

---

15. *Luther's Works*, 40:34–35.
16. From Luther's Confession of March 1528, cited in Gene Edward Veith, "Our Calling and God's Glory," *Modern Reformation* 16, no. 6 (2007): 22–28, accessed October 6, 2015, http://www.modernreformation.org/default.php?page=articledisplay &var2=881.

and clerks are "doing a holy work and [are] members of a holy order."

Sacrifices Relocated

Along with a redefinition of priesthood was a redefinition of sacrifice. What sacrifice do these Protestant priests offer to God? Not the Mass. The atoning sacrifice of Christ is a finished work. It is complete and cannot be added to, nor does it need any extension. So instead of offering Christ again in the Mass to secure God's grace, the Protestant priests offer *themselves* in response to God's mercy (Rom. 12:1). We are not securing God's favor through a repetition of Christ's sacrifice. We are responding to God's favor in Christ through the offering of our lives in gratitude. Luther writes:

> In the New Testament there is no sacrifice except the one which is common to all, namely the one described in Rom. 12[:1], where Paul teaches us to present our bodies as a sacrifice, just as Christ sacrificed his body for us on the cross. In this sacrifice he includes the offering of praise and thanksgiving. Peter likewise commands in 1 Pet. 2[:5] that we offer spiritual sacrifices acceptable to God through Jesus Christ, that is, ourselves, not gold or animals. . . . In the church there is only this sacrifice, namely, our body. For today no other sacrifice is possible than that which is sacrificed and perfected by the Word of God, and since the Word (as we said) is common to all, the sacrifice too must be one pertaining to all.[17]

But Luther also relocated the *place* of sacrifice. No longer does it take place at an altar in a church. Indeed there is a sense in which this is the one place it does not occur. Instead we offer

---

17. *Luther's Works*, 40:28–29.

our lives to God in whatever context he has placed us. Everywhere becomes holy ground. Everyday life is the sacred place where we offer sacrifices of thanksgiving to God.

Retreating from the world, far from making it easier to please God, makes it harder, for then you have no time to fulfill the roles God has assigned to you.

> Are you a husband, and you think you have not enough to do in that sphere to govern your wife, children, domestics, and property so that all may be obedient to God and you do no one any harm? Yea, if you had five heads and ten hands, even then you would be too weak for your task, so that you would never dare to think of making a pilgrimage or doing any kind of saintly work.[18]

Vocation

The word "calling" or "vocation" was used in the medieval period to describe religious orders and sacred ministry. Luther took the term and reapplied it to the activity of all Christians in whatever context they found themselves. Indeed those who believe you could best serve God in a monastery reject their true "call" to serve others and instead opt for their own private worship. Luther's key text was 1 Corinthians 7:20: "Each one should remain in the condition in which he was called."

COCREATION

When we pray the Lord's Prayer, we ask God to give us our daily bread. And he does. But the normal way he provides this is not through manna appearing from heaven, as he did for

---

18. Martin Luther, "Sermon on John 21:19–24," in *The Precious and Sacred Writings of Martin Luther*, ed. John Lenker, vol. 10 (Minneapolis: Lutherans in All Lands, 1905), 242, cited in Marc Kolden, "Luther on Vocation," *Word & World* 3, no. 4 (1983): 386.

the Israelites in the wilderness. Normally he does it through farmers, millers, and bakers. If I buy my daily bread from a supermarket, does that mean God has not provided it? Should I be giving thanks to Walmart instead of God? Luther's answer is that *God provides* bread *through* the farmer, miller, and baker.

God's work of creation is not just his original act of bringing the world into existence—he works as Creator to sustain his world. But he does this sustaining work through the actions of human beings. We are cocreators with God. This, of course, gives great significance to the work of the farmers, millers, and bakers. Their work is an act of cocreation. They are cooperating with God. God is milking the cows through the vocation of the milkmaid, says Luther. Vocation is a "mask of God." We see the milkmaid. But behind the milkmaid is the work of God.

Vocation is not just about how one earns one's living. God could have chosen to populate the world as he did in the beginning by bringing people forth from the dust. But instead he chose to create new human life through the procreation of men and women. He chose to nurture children in the context of families. So the idea of vocation encompasses your role as a husband or wife, as a father or mother. Again God chose to protect and order human life through earthly government. So politics can be a vocation. God often heals through doctors. He creates works of beauty through artists.

A Christian businessman once said to me (Tim):

> In much Christian teaching the value of your work is only seen in moments of proclamation because work itself is not ministry. There is nothing on making a difference at work through work. Or else value is given to jobs that affect quality of life through public service (teachers, nurses), but not wealth creation. Many working Christians have no positive feedback at the end of the day. No moral vision for wealth

creation as that which pays for the health service as well as gospel ministry.

In contrast to this, Luther says, "What seem to be secular works are actually the praise of God and represent an obedience which is well pleasing to him." Housework may have "no obvious appearance of holiness, yet those very household chores are more to be valued than all the works of monks and nuns."[19] We do not need to leave the world and go into a monastery to serve God. We glorify God in all of life. There is no hierarchy of professions in God's sight. "Our Saviour Christ," said the English Reformer Hugh Latimer (ca. 1487–1555),

> was a carpenter, and got his living with great labour. Therefore let no man disdain to follow him in a common calling and occupation. For as he blessed our nature with taking upon him the shape of man, so in his doing he blessed all occupations and arts.[20]

STATION AND CALLING

One of the strengths of Luther's doctrine is the value it gives to the activity of unbelievers while adding extra impetus to Christians. Luther uses two different words for our social activities: "station" (*Stand*) and "calling" or "vocation" (*Beruf*). Everyone has a station in life, believer and unbeliever. We all have a place God has assigned to us. As we act within those stations, we all contribute to God's providential care of the world.

But, in response to God's Word, Christians see their station as a calling from God. We understand our station to be a call from God to glorify him and serve others. What transforms a

---

19. Cited in Alister McGrath, *Roots That Refresh: A Celebration of Reformation Spirituality* (London: Hodder & Stoughton, 1991), 141.
20. Cited in ibid., 143.

station into a calling is faith. By faith we see our daily activities as tasks given to us by God to be done for his glory and for the common good.

Many Christians struggle to find a sense of calling. To this Luther says, "How is it possible that you are not called? You have always been in some state or station; you have always been a husband or wife, or boy or girl, or servant."[21] Luther would not have understood the language of "finding your calling." Your calling is not mysterious or difficult to discern. It is the current circumstances of your life. If you are a mother, then it is being a mother. If you are an office worker, then it is being an office worker. There is a freedom to change, but there is not a mysterious word from God waiting to be discovered to mandate your change. Your responsibility is to serve your neighbor in your current context.

By now it should be clear that vocation for Luther is much more than simply a call to do your job well. Today the term "vocation" is used narrowly to mean your profession or job. So, for example, we use the phrase "vocational training," which means training for a job as opposed to training for some other purpose. But Luther used the term to describe every social activity or function. And it is a call not just to fulfill our responsibilities well, but also to see God at work throughout human social interactions. Gene Edward Veith comments:

> For a Christian, conscious of vocation as the mask of God, all of life, even the most mundane facets of our existence, become occasions to glorify God. Whenever someone does something for you—brings your meal at a restaurant, cleans up after you, builds your house, preaches a sermon—be grateful for the human beings whom God is using to bless

---

21. Luther, "Sermon on John 21:19–24," 242, cited in Kolden, "Luther on Vocation," 386.

you and praise him for his unmerited gifts. Do you savor your food? Glorify God for the hands that prepared it. Are you moved by a work of art—a piece of music, a novel, a movie? Glorify God who has given such artistic gifts to human beings.[22]

There are dangers in the way an understanding of vocations can be applied. First, it can lead to a passive acceptance of the status quo, however unjust that may be. If you find yourself in a job where you are poorly treated, should you stay in it because this is God's calling on your life? To say you are called to stay is a misreading of Luther. His point is not that you *may* not change your role, but that you *need* not. You do not have to stop being a baker and become a monk if you truly want to serve God. You can serve God just as well as a baker. But if you have the opportunity to change your role, then so be it—as long as it is a legitimate, lawful role and as long as you undertake the new role with the same sense of vocation.

Second, it can lead to an attitude that confuses serving God with serving your boss. If you fulfill your calling in the workplace by doing a good job, then that may be taken as a justification for doing whatever your boss tells you. That in turn has the potential to create the kinds of excuses for immoral behavior exemplified by the cry "I was just obeying orders!" The better an employee you are, it may be supposed, the better a Christian. There is some truth in this. The issue, however, is who defines what it means to be a "good" employee. For Luther, fulfilling your calling in any sphere is defined by love for neighbor. So the authority of your boss is always relativized by a commitment to the common good.

But perhaps the greatest danger we face is a secularized

---

22. Veith, "Our Calling and God's Glory," 22–28.

version of justification by works.[23] In Luther's day someone was likely to spend his or her whole life in the same job. Today people expect to change jobs and even professions several times during their lives. Here the doctrine of justification becomes vital. Identity is found not in success at work; it is given to us in Christ by grace. If we think of calling without God, then work itself becomes an idol or a means of self-justification.

People often talk about the "Protestant work ethic"—the commitment to work that arose because of the Reformation emphasis on everyday life. Today the Protestant work ethic is often blamed for the overworked and overstressed culture of modern life. Work became a good thing, and so the more work, the better. But work was never ultimate in the thinking of the Reformation. God was ultimate. We work to the glory of God and rest to his glory. So Sabbath rest also became an important theme in Reformation churches.

The real problem is the removal of God. In the modern world work has become an end in itself. Indeed, in many ways it has become a god, offering salvation in the form of self-fulfillment. We look to find meaning or our sense of worth through work itself. Robert Banks concludes:

> The pressure of time in everyday life is not primarily the result of the development or distribution of clocks and watches. More significant were changes in worldview leading to a less God-centred and grace-based approach to life in favour of a more man-centred and work-justifying attitude.[24]

The information revolution has accelerated this. It offers more potential for "self-actualization" through work. Most jobs cre-

---

23. See Tim Chester, *The Busy Christian's Guide to Busyness*, 2nd ed. (Leicester: Inter-Varsity Press, 2008); Chester, *Gospel-Centred Work* (London: Good Book, 2013).
24. Robert Banks, *The Tyranny of Time* (Leicester: Inter-Varsity Press, 1983), 126.

ated in the Industrial Revolution were relatively dull. Their value lay in the income they earned for your family and the service they rendered to your neighbor. But now we compete for "rewarding" jobs that are intrinsically fulfilling.

The Reformation still matters. For this new "work ethic" departs from the Reformation theology in two important ways. First, the new work ethic is self-justifying. The salvation by works of medieval Catholicism has been replaced with salvation by work. And salvation is now defined as self-fulfillment. But it is still an attempt at self-salvation. And it still does not work, which is why so many people in our culture are stressed. The elite find a form of salvation through the fulfillment and respect their jobs provide. The rest of us work all the harder to be "saved."

Second, the new work ethic is self-serving. Work is judged not by the service it renders to others but by the service it renders to me, the worker. A "good" job is defined as a job I find fulfilling rather than a job that serves the common good. When we speak of a "rewarding" job, the reward is enjoyed by the worker rather than by the community. Being a road sweeper is not seen as a good or rewarding job in our culture. But Luther would have called it a good and rewarding job because the community is rewarded with the common good of clean streets. God cleans the streets through the road sweeper, so the road sweeper is a cocreator.

Coram Deo

In medieval Catholicism God is in the monastery and not in the market place. God is in the Mass and not in the home. The more you stress the sacredness of sacred places, the less God is a feature of everyday life. It is not that God is absent. He is still there to see and count your sins. But in medieval Catholicism God was a distant and forbidding reality. He was accessed, if at all, through the mediation of the saints. You were never acceptable to him, so you would not think yourself able to approach him directly, nor would you want to.

Justification by faith means God is not distant, for Christ brings us into a relationship with God. Now God is near and God is welcoming. So this leads to a strong sense that you live life *coram Deo*, "before God." This is an important phrase for Luther. In Calvin, too, there is a strong sense of the presence of God. Calvin said that in every dimension of life human beings have "business with God," *negotium cum Deo*.[25]

Still today Christians can give the impression that true Christian work is work done for a church or parachurch. Or we think we need to go on a retreat to be truly spiritual. The very term "retreat" is a bit of a giveaway. It suggests that monastic thinking still lingers in our minds. Or we measure commitment to Christ in terms of commitment to the activities of our church. The person who regularly attends the prayer meeting and serves a church committee is assumed to be a strong Christian. People who have less time for these things because they are busy at work or serving in the community are assumed to be failing as disciples. We make the call to follow Christ a call to participate in church programs. And then we wonder why we are so poor at reaching the lost or impacting our culture.

Still, today we tend to look for religion in the extraordinary. We expect to encounter God in the special meetings in special locations, whether that is the grandeur of a cathedral with its elaborate liturgy or the buzz of a high-octane worship service. Luther's doctrine of vocation placed the work of God firmly

---

25. Calvin, *Institutes*, 1.17.2, 3.3.16, 3.7.2.

in the ordinary. Through our vocation God is revealed even in mundane activities.

God is the God of all creation. He is the God of Monday mornings as well as Sunday mornings. Humanity was made in the image of God to reflect his glory in his world. In the gospel we are restored to our true humanity. We are renewed so that we can again reflect God's glory in God's world. The Reformation affirmation of everyday life is an invitation to see the whole earth as the theater of God's glory and to see our whole lives as opportunities to reflect that glory.

11

Joy and Glory

Does the Reformation Still Matter?

Some 120 years after the Reformation got going, some 120 scholars assembled in Westminster to write the necessary documents for a reformed church in England. The first question and answer of their Westminster Shorter Catechism is a beautiful, prize flower of Reformation thought:

> *Question:* What is the chief end of man?
> *Answer:* Man's chief end is to glorify God, and to enjoy him forever.

The glory of God and enjoyment of him: these inseparable, twin truths were guiding lights for the Reformation. The Reformers held that through all the doctrines they had fought for and upheld, God was glorified and people were given comfort and joy.

Through justification by grace alone, through faith alone in Christ, God was glorified as utterly merciful and good, as both supremely holy and compassionate—and therefore people could find their comfort and delight in him. Through union with Christ believers could know a firm standing before God, gleefully knowing him as their "Abba," confident that he was powerful to save and keep to the uttermost. Without a priestly hierarchy detached from the world, believers could all call each other "brother" and "sister," living every part of life for the kind Father they had been brought to enjoy.

It has been our belief in this book that the Reformers were right in this, and *therefore the Reformation still matters*, for through these truths lives can still blossom under the joy-giving light of God's glory.

Fear and Presumption

A good test case of this can be seen in how differently Roman Catholic and Reformation theologies thought of our assurance of salvation. Can a believer *know* she is saved?

On the side of the Reformation the Puritan Richard Sibbes argued that without such assurance we simply cannot live Christian lives as God would have us live. God, he said, wants us to be thankful, cheerful, rejoicing, and strong in faith. But we shall be none of these things unless we are *sure* that God and Christ are ours for good.

> There be many duties and dispositions that God requires which we can not be in without assurance of salvation on good grounds. What is that? God bids us be thankful in all things. How can I know that, unless I *know* God is mine and Christ is mine? . . . God enjoineth us to rejoice. "Rejoice, and again I say, rejoice," Philip, iv. 4. Can a man rejoice that his name is written in heaven, and not *know* his name is written there? . . .

Alas! how can I perform cheerful service to God, when I doubt whether he be *my* God and Father or no? . . . God requires a disposition in us *that we should be full of encouragements, and strong in the Lord*; and that we should be courageous for his cause in withstanding his enemies and our enemies. How *can* there be courage in resisting our corruptions, Satan's temptations? How *can* there be courage in suffering persecution and crosses in the world, if there be not some particular interest we have in Christ and in God?[1]

Yet the very confidence that Sibbes upheld as a Christian privilege was damned by Roman Catholic theology as the sin of presumption. It was precisely one of the charges made *against* Joan of Arc at her trial in 1431. There the judges proclaimed:

This woman sins when she says she is as certain of being received into Paradise as if she were already a partaker of . . . glory, seeing that on this earthly journey no pilgrim knows if he is worthy of glory or of punishment, which the sovereign judge alone can tell.[2]

That judgment made complete sense within the logic of the system. If we can enter heaven only because we have (by God's enabling grace) become personally worthy of it, *of course* nobody can be sure. By that line of reasoning, I can only have as much confidence in heaven as I have confidence in my own sinlessness.

But while such thinking *made sense* in Roman Catholicism, it bred fear, not joy. The need to have personal merit before God left people terrified at the prospect of judgment. You can still feel it when you see a medieval fresco of the Last Judgment. You

---

1. Richard Sibbes, "A Heavenly Conference," in *The Complete Works of Richard Sibbes*, ed. Alexander B. Grosart, 7 vols. (Edinburgh: James Nichol, 1862–1864), 6:479–80 (emphases added).
2. *The Trial of Jeanne d'Arc*, trans. W. P. Barrett (New York: Gotham House, 1932), 320–21.

can hear it in the words of the *Dies Irae* that would be chanted in every Catholic Mass for the dead:

> Day of wrath, day that will dissolve the world into burning coals. . . . What am I the wretch then to say? what patron I to beseech? when scarcely the just be secure. King of tremendous Majesty. . . . do not lose me on that day. . . . My prayers are not worthy, but do Thou, Good (God), deal kindly lest I burn in perennial fire.

This was exactly why the young Luther shook with fear at the thought of death, and why he said he *hated* God (instead of enjoying him). He *could not* be thankful, cheerful, rejoicing, and strong in faith, since he believed only in God as a judge who was against him. It was a view of God reinforced by a carving he would pass underneath every time he entered the city church in Wittenberg.

> On a stone relief above the entrance to the cemetery surrounding the church, Luther saw, carved into the mandorla (an aureole shaped like an almond), Christ seated on the rainbow as judge of the world, so angry the veins stand out, menacing and swollen, on his forehead.[3]

With his discovery that sinners are freely declared righteous in Christ, that all changed. No longer was his confidence for that day placed in himself: it all rested on Christ and *his* sufficient righteousness. And so the horrifying doomsday became for him what he would call "the most happy Last Day," the day of Jesus, his friend.[4] The consolation it brought to all who held

---

3. Oswald Bayer, "Justification: Basis and Boundary of Theology," in *By Faith Alone: Essays in Honor of Gerhard O. Forde*, ed. Joseph A. Burgess and Marc Kolden (Grand Rapids, MI: Eerdmans, 2004), 78.

4. *D. Martin Luthers Werke: Kritische Gesamtausgabe*, 127 vols. (Weimar: Böhlau, 1883–2009), 53:401, cited in Paul Althaus, *The Theology of Martin Luther* (Philadelphia: Fortress, 1966), 420–21.

to Reformation theology was captured perfectly in the striking wording of the Heidelberg Catechism's question and answer:

> *Question:* What *comfort* is it to you that Christ will come to judge the living and the dead?
> *Answer:* In all my sorrow and persecution, I lift up my head and eagerly await as judge from heaven the very same person who before has submitted himself to the judgment of God for my sake, and has removed all the curse from me.[5]

Comfort in Christ for the struggling believer: *that* was the theology of the Reformation.

Purgatory

What happens to us after death was no sideshow issue for the Reformation. Luther's very first skirmish—that October day in 1517 when he nailed his ninety-five theses to the church door—concerned purgatory. Purgatory provided relief for the problem that nobody would die righteous enough to have merited salvation fully. It was (and is) often viewed as a halfway house between heaven and hell—nowhere near as good as heaven, but not so bad as hell. But purgatory was meant to be a place exclusively for the saved. It was the place where Christian souls would go after death to have all their sins slowly purged from them. Through time in purgatory sinners would be purified and finally made fit for heaven.

The doctrine of purgatory had got into full swing in the late Middle Ages, and fear of the place began to spawn a vast purgatory industry. Prayers and Masses would be said for souls in purgatory, and special "chantries" were founded, with priests dedicated to saying those prayers and Masses for fortunate

---

5. Heidelberg Catechism, question 52 (emphasis added).

(wealthy) souls. And then, of course, there were indulgences: awards of merit handed out by the church to those who had earned (or bought) them. These indulgences could "top up" an individual's own personal merit before God, thus fast-tracking them through purgatory, or even allowing them to leapfrog purgatory altogether (with a "full," or "plenary," indulgence). It was an indulgence monger, Johann Tetzel, who stung Luther into action with his blood-chilling religious marketeering.

None of this has really disappeared from modern Roman Catholicism. The *Catechism of the Catholic Church* still affirms belief in purgatory and indulgences. Indeed, when Pope Benedict XVI wrote about the last things, he gave more pages to considering purgatory than to heaven and hell combined.[6] And why not? When justification is thought of as a process of growth in righteousness (as it is in Roman Catholicism), purgatory and indulgences make sense. Without the righteousness of Christ given to us, how else can anyone be righteous enough for heaven, unless they have much more time to grow than this short life affords?

But to the Reformers purgatory quickly came to symbolize all that was wrong with the Roman Catholic view of salvation. John Calvin argued clearly and bluntly that

> purgatory is a deadly fiction of Satan, which nullifies the cross of Christ, inflicts unbearable contempt upon God's mercy, and overturns and destroys our faith. For what means this purgatory of theirs but that satisfaction for sins is paid by the souls of the dead after their death? Hence, when the notion of satisfaction is destroyed, purgatory itself is straightway torn up by the very roots. But if it is perfectly clear from our preceding discourse that the blood

---

6. Joseph Ratzinger, *Eschatology: Death and Eternal Life*, 2nd ed., trans. Michael Waldstein (Washington, DC: Catholic University of America Press, 1988).

of Christ is the sole satisfaction for the sins of believers, the sole expiation, the sole purgation, what remains but to say that purgatory is simply a dreadful blasphemy against Christ?[7]

Calvin's logic is simple: purgatory strips Christ of his glory as a merciful and fully sufficient Savior; it also destroys any confident joy in us. No joy, no glory: purgatory went entirely against the grain of Reformation thought, which cared so passionately about those twin prizes.

A Protestant Purgatory?

And yet, while Protestants have almost unanimously been averse to the idea of purgatory since the earliest days of the Reformation, things are changing. One of the darlings of modern evangelicalism, C. S. Lewis, was as winsome as ever when he turned his pen in support of some form of purgatory in *The Great Divorce* and *Letters to Malcolm*. He and others have made many think again with arguments that are as revealing as they are appealing.

Jerry Walls has assembled what is probably the most thorough case for a Protestant acceptance of purgatory, and his argument is worth hearing.[8] Walls actually *agrees* with Calvin's classic argument against purgatory, but suggests there is another way to think of purgatory without falling afoul of Calvin's anathema. That is, purgatory could be thought of *not* as a place to pay off any remaining debt uncovered by the blood of Christ, *but instead* as a place where those who are already forgiven might go to become fully holy and so fit for heaven. In other words, purgatory should be seen not as a place of punish-

---

7. Calvin, *Institutes*, 3.5.6.
8. Jerry L. Walls, *Purgatory: The Logic of Total Transformation* (New York: Oxford University Press, 2012).

ment but as a school where the taste for holiness is cultivated such that graduates might fully enjoy heaven, instead of feeling out of place. There in purgatory Christians will not get more forgiven (their forgiveness is complete), but they will get acclimatized to the holy atmosphere of heaven.

To illustrate, both Walls and Lewis turn to John Henry Newman's poem *The Dream of Gerontius*, the account of a soul's journey from death to judgment and then purgatory. Near the end, the soul approaches the throne of God (and in order to appreciate the pathos of the moment, it is worth listening to Edward Elgar's musical rendition of *The Dream*). At that point the full orchestra blares out the terrifying holiness of God, and in pitiful strains the soul cries out to be sent away to purgatory, unable to bear the dazzling brightness of God's presence:

> Take me away, and in the lowest deep
> There let me be,
> And there in hope the lone night-watches keep,
> Told out for me.
> There, motionless and happy in my pain,
> Lone, not forlorn,—
> There will I sing my sad perpetual strain,
> Until the morn.
> There will I sing, and soothe my stricken breast,
> Which ne'er can cease
> To throb, and pine, and languish, till possest
> Of its Sole Peace.
> There will I sing my absent Lord and Love:—
> Take me away,
> That sooner I may rise, and go above,
> And see Him in the truth of everlasting day.[9]

---

9. John Henry Newman, *The Dream of Gerontius* (Staten Island, NY: St Pauls/Alba House, 2001), 68.

Now Lewis and Walls may have sidestepped Calvin's volley, but there remains something entirely incompatible with Reformation thought here. True, purgatory is not now meant to finish off the work of the cross in securing our atonement. The problem has to do with some of those other basic questions we have seen raised by the Reformation: What does God give us? Himself, or some other thing called "grace"? What is our new life? Knowing him, or being enabled by him for something else? Here in *The Dream* the soul thinks (and we are clearly meant to agree) that holiness and transformation will best happen *away* from the presence of God. There "lone" and "absent" from the Lord, self-soothing, the soul believes it will best mature. Apparently absence makes the heart grow fonder, even in eternity.

The soul's logic is at complete odds with all we have seen— that we find our joy and ourselves transformed *through our communion with God, by glorying in him.* Our sanctification is not something God ever enables from a distance with hands off. We find ourselves "transformed into the same image from one degree of glory to another" *precisely as we* "contemplate the Lord's glory" (2 Cor. 3:18). Finally, when he appears, "we shall be like him, *because we shall see him* as he is" (1 John 3:2).

The soul claims to be "*happy* in my pain," but the overwhelming tone of what it cries is one aching, stricken, "*sad* perpetual strain." That is where any purgatory must leave it: belief in purgatory brings sadness and discomfort. Reformation thought, on the other hand, always sees joy found in the glory of God. True happiness is found pressing *into* (not away from) the brightness that purifies and heals.

S. D. G.

What the Reformers saw, especially through the message of justification by faith alone, was the revelation of an exuberantly happy God who glories in sharing his happiness. He is not stingy or utilitarian, but a God who glories in being gracious. (That is why, according to Rom. 4:20, dependent faith glorifies him.) To steal from his glory by claiming any credit for ourselves would only steal our own joy in so marvelous a God.

And the glory of God, Calvin believed, can be seen not just in justification, the cross, and the face of Christ: the whole world, he argued, is a theater of God's glory.[10] Throughout creation we see the sheer largesse of the Creator.

> Now if we ponder to what end God created food, we shall find that he meant not only to provide for necessity but also for delight and good cheer. . . . In grasses, trees, and fruits, apart from their various uses, there is beauty of appearance and pleasantness of odor [compare Gen. 2:9]. For if this were not true, the prophet would not have reckoned them among the benefits of God, "that wine gladdens the heart of man, that oil makes his face shine" [Ps. 104:15]. . . . Has the Lord clothed the flowers with the great beauty that greets our eyes, the sweetness of smell that is wafted upon our nostrils, and yet will it be unlawful for our eyes to be affected by that beauty, or our sense of smell by the sweetness of that odor? . . . Did he not, in short, render many things attractive to us, apart from their necessary use?[11]

That is just why Johann Sebastian Bach, when satisfied with his compositions, would write on them "S. D. G." for *soli Deo gloria*, "glory to God alone." For through his music he wanted to sound out the beauty and glory of God, so pleasing both God and people. The glory of God, he believed, gratuitously rings out throughout creation, bringing joy wherever it is appreciated. And that is worth living for and promoting.

---

10. Calvin, *Commentary*, on John 13:31.
11. Calvin, *Institutes*, 3.10.2.

In fact, wrote Calvin, that is the secret of happiness and the secret of life:

> For whatever the philosophers may have ever said of the chief good, it was nothing but cold and vain, for *they confined man to himself, while it is necessary for us to go out of ourselves to find happiness.* The chief good of man is nothing else but union with God.[12]

Against everything we are told today, happiness is not found in ourselves—in appreciating our own beauty or convincing ourselves of it. Deep, lasting, satisfying happiness is found in the all-glorious God. All of which is really just another way of saying:

> *Question:* What is the chief end of man?
> *Answer:* Man's chief end is to glorify God, and to enjoy him forever.

Joy and Glory Still Matter

The only way the Reformation could possibly *not* still matter would be if beauty, goodness, truth, joy, and human flourishing no longer mattered. We have been made to enjoy God, but without the great truths the Reformers fought for that *display* him as glorious and enjoyable, we shall not do so. Seeing less of him, we shall be lesser and sadder. Seeing more of him, we shall be fuller and happier. And on that note we should leave the last words to John Calvin. This is why the Reformation still matters:

> It will not suffice simply to hold that there is One whom all ought to honor and adore, unless we are also persuaded that he is the fountain of every good, and that we must seek

---

12. Calvin, *Commentary*, on Heb. 4:10 (emphasis added).

nothing elsewhere than in him. . . . For until men recognize that they owe everything to God, that they are nourished by his fatherly care, that he is the Author of their every good, that they should seek nothing beyond him—they will never yield him willing service. Nay, unless they establish their complete happiness in him, they will never give themselves truly and sincerely to him.[13]

---

13. Calvin, *Institutes*, 1.2.1.

General Index

Scripture Index